YES, GOD CAN!

To Renee,

May the Lord bless you.

Sincerely,

Caroline D. Snyder

YES, GOD CAN!

The Demonstration of the *Miraculous*
Power of an Awesome GOD

CAROLINE D. SNYDER

TATE PUBLISHING
AND ENTERPRISES, LLC

Published by Tate Publishing & Enterprises, LLC
127 E. Trade Center Terrace | Mustang, Oklahoma 73064 USA
1.888.361.9473 | www.tatepublishing.com

Tate Publishing is committed to excellence in the publishing industry. The company reflects the philosophy established by the founders, based on Psalm 68:11,
"The Lord gave the word and great was the company of those who published it."

Book design copyright © 2013 by Tate Publishing, LLC. All rights reserved.
Cover design by Rodrigo Adolfo
Interior design by Jomar Ouano

Published in the United States of America

ISBN: 978-1-62854-989-8
Biography & Autobiography / Personal Memoirs
13.09.06

This book is filled with miracles that God performed in the life of my family. It is written to encourage others to believe that nothing is impossible with God if you only believe.

Catherine Shumaker

DEDICATION

I would like to dedicate this book to my Mom, Catherine Riddell Cooksey Shumaker.

This book came about because of her love for God and her love for passing on her faith and sharing her life with her family. All three of her children learned to love her Jesus because she not only taught us her faith but she lived it.

She was a woman of God. The principles she lived by were those taught to her from the Word of God. She made living the Christian life an exciting adventure. Her life was not about religion but about a personal relationship with a personal God.

I honor her today. I am so thankful to God for the privilege of being placed under her guidance and for all the selfless love she showed to all she ministered to.

I am the woman I am today because of her great love and instruction to me and my siblings.

I pray this book will be a blessing to you as you read the stories of our family. I thank God for all the awesome miracles he has performed and his wonderful care to all of us.

Acknowledgments

I would like to thank God for allowing me to put on paper all the wonderful miracles God has done for me and my family over the years. His goodness and mercy and loving kindness overwhelms me. From the beginning of my writing, I asked the Holy Spirit to be my senior partner and I believe he has been faithful to me all along the way. To God be all the honor and glory.

Along this journey I want to sincerely thank my husband, Marvin, for all of the encouragement he has given to me to write this book. He has read and re-read each page, made corrections and copied and recopied many a page to get this manuscript ready to go to the next step on the way to having it published. I am so glad God has given me such a wonderful husband, co-worker and friend to help me accomplish the dreams God has put in my heart. Marvin has prayed daily for me as I wrote and rewrote these chapters, and without his encouragement, I am sure this task would not have been completed. Thank you, Marvin.

I would like to thank our children for all of their support and prayers, and for encouraging me to tell not only my story but allowing me to tell their stories as well so that others can be encouraged and grow in the Lord.

I would like to sincerely thank Carol Kenzy for the hours she put in correcting my grammar and proofreading my work. It was a painstaking job of love and I appreciate all her help and prayers for my success.

Flo Whittaker also was a blessing to me as she edited my work to get it ready for the publisher, and she gave me sound advice as one who has edited many books and knew the flaws of a first time writer. Thank you, Flo, for all the hours you spent getting this book ready for publication and all of your sound advice. She also gave me the name of Tate Publishing Company which I will forever be grateful for.

I would like to thank my friends who have prayed for this book to be published and who believed that it would happen and that it would be used as a tool to win people to Christ and encourage those who need a miracle in their lives. Thank you also for the testimonies that you allowed me to share along with those of my family. I know they will be a blessing to all who read them.

I would sincerely like to thank Chet Ricewick who helped us with all the computer work needed to get this manuscript ready to go to the publishers. Without him we would have had a difficult journey.

Our niece Gylene Snyder took some of the photographs and then scanned the rest to get the photographic portion of the manuscript up to par to submit. Without her I don't know what we would have done. God surely sent the right people to us to get this work done for which we are forever grateful. Thank you, Gylene!

A sincere thank you to all the people who worked on my book at Tate Publishing House. I feel so privileged that you chose my book for publication. May God bless each one that made my book a success.

Lastly, I would like to thank each one of you who buys this book. I have asked the Lord to bless you and encourage you and to perform miracles in your lives. Truly, I believe all things are possible to those who believe.

CONTENTS

Introduction

For many years, I have hidden in my heart and shared with others the many miracles God has performed in my family. Growing up, my mother would tell us many exciting stories of miracles God had done for us. She instilled in us the greatness of God and told us if we believed, nothing was impossible with God.

She always wanted to honor God and write a book telling these true stories to encourage others to believe that God is the same yesterday, today and forever. She never got the opportunity to put on paper what she shared by word of mouth with anyone who would listen. I believe that God is giving me this awesome opportunity to fulfill my mother's dream.

> Therefore, shall ye lay up these my words in your heart and in your soul, and bind them for a sign upon your hand, that they may be as frontlets between your eyes.
>
> And ye shall teach them your children speaking of them when thou sittest in thine house, and when thou walkest by the way, when thou liest down, and when thou risest up.

And thou shalt write them upon the door posts of thine house and upon thy gates.

That your days may be multiplied, and the days of your children, in the land which the Lord sware unto your fathers to give them, as the days of heaven upon the earth. Deuteronomy 11:18-21 (KJV)

Wherever the Israelites went, God encouraged them to make memorials of his great acts and to pass these stories down from generation to generation so that all would know how great God is.

"And thou shalt teach them diligently unto thy children, and shalt talk to them when thou sittest in thine house, and when thou walkest by the way, and when thou liest down, and when thou risest up." Deuteronomy 6:7 (KJV)

The Bible is full of the awesome acts of God. These stories encourage us, excite us and fill us with hope.

"Jesus Christ the same yesterday, and today, and forever." Hebrews 13:8 (KJV)

So many prophets have declared that 2012 is going to be the year when we are going to see God answer our prayers. We are going to see great and mighty things happening as God shows his people his great favor.

It is my desire to write about the rich heritage of the demonstration of the power of God shown to my family, and pass these true stories along to you that you might believe for your own miracles.

God loves us so much and is ready and able to meet our every need. He is waiting for us to ask in faith, without doubting, so that we might receive all he has for us. May this book inspire you to do just that.

I hope this is a book that you won't be able to put down! We serve a wonderful, exciting God who is ready to declare his wonders to all who will have an ear to hear and a heart to believe and a mind to accept.

"O God, thou hast taught me from my youth: and hitherto have I declared thy wondrous works." Psalm 71:17 (KJV)

I fully desire to do what it tells us in Psalm 26:7

That I may publish with the voice of thanksgiving, and tell of all thy wondrous works." Psalm 26:7 (KJV)

May God bless you, inspire you and use you to affect your world with how great our God is!

Sincerely in Christ,
Caroline Correa Snyder

ENGLAND 1919–1933

"We will not hide them from their children, shewing to the generation to come the praises of the Lord, and his strength, and his wonderful works that he hath done." Psalm 78:4 (KJV)

I have been blessed with a rich Christian heritage. The Bible says that, for those that love the Lord, their children will be blessed from generation to generation. I can truly say that has been the story in my family. That does not mean we have never had a problem or a difficulty. Nor does it mean that God gave us everything we prayed for and answered our prayers the way we would have liked to see them answered. God sometimes gives us a "no," sometimes a "yes" and sometimes a "wait."

I grew up believing:

> "For my thoughts are not your thoughts, neither are your ways my ways, saith the Lord.
>
> For as the heavens are higher than the earth, so are my ways higher than your ways and my thoughts than your thoughts." Isaiah 55:8-9 (KJV)

Although we do not always understand the why, one thing I know is that God's ways are higher than our ways and his ways are the best. I know also that he is never late with his answers and that he always has my best interest at heart in all his dealings with me.

The true stories in this book that were passed down from generation to generation declare the almighty power of God. Family blessings are my heritage and I pass them on to my children and generations to come. The Bible says that there is power in your words.

"Death and life are in the power of the tongue: and they that love it shall eat the fruit thereof." Proverbs 18:21 (KJV)

So today, I bless my children with the blessing of the righteous. I will declare the goodness of God in the land of the living.

My story starts with the birth of my mother, Catherine Smith. She was born on December 21, 1919 in Yorkshire, England. She had a happy childhood, growing up with two older brothers, Jack and Rupert. Her father was a postman and her mother was a homemaker. They taught their children to honor and love God and as a family, attended the Methodist Church.

THE BEGINNING OF MIRACLES: GOD RE-CREATES A LEG BONE:

The first story Catherine told us about God's miraculous power was taken from her childhood. Growing up, she was a tomboy and was always joining her brothers and their friends in games of football (soccer is called football in England). Her brothers did not always welcome her presence. But, since she was a strong-willed child, she often got her own way. One fateful day, while playing football, one of the boys kicked her very hard in her leg.

After this accident, she had a lot of pain in that leg. Some time had passed and she was still complaining of pain, so her mother took her to the doctor. Since Catherine had a hard time putting any weight on her leg, the doctor ordered x-rays. My grandparents were told that the kick had damaged her bone; it had started to disintegrate. After several months of doctors' appointments and more x-rays, my grandparents were instructed that Catherine was not to stand on this leg as the disease in the bone was going further up her leg. They put an iron brace on her leg and put her in a wheelchair. After some time, the doctors told my grandparents that they could not stop the progress of the disease. Catherine would have to have her leg amputated and so the operation was scheduled.

Coming home from the doctor's appointment, Catherine saw an advertisement on a poster board that showed a lame man throwing his crutches away. It was advertising a healing service. Being an inquisitive child, she asked her mother what that meant. My grandmother explained to her that in Jesus's day, sick people would come to him and he would heal them. Catherine declared she wanted Jesus to do that for her too. She wanted to attend the advertised healing crusade.

When they got home, Catherine the apple of her father's eye, begged her dad to tell her mother to take her to the service. My grandmother did not want to go because she did not believe God still healed. Catherine, however, cried and begged her father to let her go. He said to my grandmother, "She is going to have her leg off next week, so why don't you just take her instead of having her get so upset." My grandmother gave in and took Catherine the following evening to the service.

When they arrived, my grandmother found an aisle seat at the back of the church where Catherine could stay in her wheelchair in the aisle. My grandmother intended to make a quick escape as soon as the service was over.

At the end of the service, the minister made an appeal and asked anyone who would like Jesus to heal them to come up to the front of the church. Catherine was a little girl but she had a big voice. She cried out loudly, "I want Jesus to heal me!" My grandmother was so embarrassed by this and told her to be quiet. When Catherine continued to make a fuss, she scolded her and told her that they were leaving. However, there was an usher who was standing close by and he said, "I'll take your little girl up front for you if you would like." Catherine cried out a big thank you and my grandmother said a resounding *"No!"* By this time, Catherine was making such a loud noise and fuss about going up for prayer that my grandmother turned red in the face, thoroughly embarrassed as people were turning around in their seats to see who was making all the noise. To stop the commotion, she gave the usher permission to push her wheelchair up to the front and my grandmother sheepishly followed behind.

At the front of the church, the minister was praying a simple prayer to Jesus to heal the people who had come up for healing. When he got to Catherine, he said, "Little girl, do you believe Jesus can heal your leg?" Catherine said, "Yes, just like he did in that picture of the man throwing away his crutches!" The minister then prayed for her and said, "Now, we are going to take this iron brace off your leg and help you stand and walk in Jesus's name." When he said this to her, my grandmother, who had been standing quietly next to the wheelchair said, "Oh no, you don't! The doctor said if she tries to stand on that leg, the disease will go further up her leg. Instead of the amputation being at the knee, it could go higher and she could lose her life." The minister looked up to my grandmother and said, "Doubting Thomas?" Catherine declared excitedly and loudly, "I believe Jesus has healed my leg!" My grandmother then allowed the brace to come off and Catherine stood up. At first, her leg was shaky and weak; but after a few steps, she ran around the church. Everyone was praising God and my grandmother was crying and thanking God for the miracle.

When they got home, my grandfather rejoiced along with the rest of the family. The next day, Catherine had a doctor's appointment. They walked into the doctor's office, pushing the wheelchair and Catherine was not wearing the brace. They were sitting, waiting for their appointment, excited to tell the doctor of the miracle. Instead of the doctor rejoicing about the news, he chastised my grandmother. He said, "You foolish woman! Don't you know that these people can hypnotize you and then a few days later your daughter could drop down dead? I told you not to let her stand on this leg. We will have to take another x-ray and see just how much more damage has been done." My grandmother was in tears and scolded Catherine, "I told you we were not supposed to take off that iron brace and now, see how angry the doctor is! We could have done more harm to you. I never should have listened to you."

It took some time after the x-ray had been taken for the doctor to come back into the room. He came in with several other doctors and they pulled and pushed on Catherine's leg. The doctor declared, "I don't know what happened, but there seems to be a perfect bone in her leg! But, if she starts with any pains again, you need to bring her right back for us to take another x-ray." On hearing this report, my grandmother was filled with courage again and declared to the doctor in a loud voice for all to hear, "I told you God had healed my child!" Catherine never had any problems in that leg in her lifetime, thanks to God's healing touch.

A GOITER DISAPPEARS!

It was during my mother's childhood that my grandfather had a miraculous healing in his body also. He had a large goiter and could not sleep on the one side because of it. One day, the pastor saw my grandfather in town as he was delivering the mail. The pastor asked him, "Mr. Smith, why do you have this large goiter on your neck?" My grandfather told the pastor he was praying and asking God to touch him but so far he still had the goiter. The minister told him to get down on his knees right on the street in the middle of town and they would pray for healing right there and then. My grandfather was well-known and he felt embarrassed to do this. He also had a holy fear of the minister so he got down on his knees. The pastor prayed for him right there with people walking around them, traffic travelling on the road and everyone looking at this strange sight. Once the minister had finished his fiery prayer, he said his goodbyes and off he went. He told my grandfather to start praising God for his healing. My grandfather got up and wondered how many folks had seen him on his knees in the middle of the street! He purposed in his heart to start thanking God for his healing even if he still had the visible goiter.

Several days later, Catherine was awakened in the early hours of the morning by my grandmother's screams. From all the noise coming from the room, Catherine thought there was an intruder and they were being attacked. She ran into the room to see what was happening. She found her parents crying and hugging one another. Apparently, my grandfather had awakened and found himself sleeping on the side he had not been able to lay on. When he felt his neck, the goiter was gone. He was so overjoyed that he grabbed my grandmother and started shaking her and shouting, "It's gone, it's gone!" My grandmother, who had been in a deep sleep, was startled. She screamed at the top of her voice and awakened the whole family. What a great time of rejoicing that must have been!

Abraham believed God for a son and the Bible says that it was counted to him for righteousness. He believed it when God had said to him that he was going to be the father of a nation. He believed this before he had a son. Even though Abraham had to wait until he was one hundred years old, God fulfilled his promise.

> As it is written I have made thee a father of many nations.) before him whom he believed, even God, who quickeneth the dead, and calleth those things which be not as though they were. Romans 4:17 (KJV)

God is good! God can work miracles in us even while we are sleeping. What a testimony for my grandfather to declare to all the people he delivered the mail to that day. I am sure this must have inspired many who knew him, to believe God for their own miracles.

ANOTHER TYPE OF MIRACLE:

The next miracle that Catherine loved to give God the glory for is not of a healing, but a miracle of God's protection.

In England, they had youth groups called Girl Guides and Boy Scouts that met after school. The younger girls' club was called Brownies. You wore a uniform, learned the word of God and also earned badges by doing good deeds and learning life skills.

One day, as Catherine was walking home, she was approached by a man who asked for directions to a certain place. Although she gave him directions, he insisted that he needed her to show him how to get there. It was not too far away and he thought he would get lost. Catherine first said she needed to get home. But, the man told her that, since she was a Brownie, it would only be right that she take him there as a good deed.

As she was taking him there, she saw her older brother at the top of the street and she called out to him to let him know where she was going. It was typical English weather, foggy with limited visibility. When she called out to Jack, the man picked her up and ran around the corner. Jack heard the cry but thought it must have been an uncle she was with and did not think any more about it. Later when he got home, Jack was alarmed because Catherine was nowhere to be found.

Meanwhile, this man asked Catherine where she lived. She said as a child she was usually honest but for some reason she gave her cousin's address which was on the opposite side of town. The man forced her to walk with him to an area which was known as "the Hollows." This was a large open space of land where sand had been deposited with sand piles and sand pits everywhere.

Unbeknownst to the kidnapper, this area was located at the top of the street where Catherine's true address was. When he got her there, he started to try to undress her and molest her. He exposed himself. She also saw that he had a knife.

By this time, Jack was surprised that his little sister was not home yet. His mother did not know of any uncle that Catherine could have been with, so they and their neighbors searched for her, calling out her name. In those days, everyone knew their neighbors and they would look out for one another. The mothers were all homemakers and families were close knit. The neighborhood was like a big family. Catherine and her captor heard everyone calling her name. She was struggling to get away from this man that had her in one of the sand pits. He ran off when he saw the flashlights and heard the people shouting her name getting closer.

Of course, the police were called in and her father took her to the police station to look through books to see if she could identify this man. They found out he had attacked several other children. It was only God's hand of protection and mercy on Catherine that kept her from being raped and possibly murdered.

One day, Catherine was walking down the street with her father when she saw this man selling newspapers on the street corner. She was so petrified that she squeezed her father's hand really tight. Her father asked her what was wrong, but she could not say anything until they were around the corner. When she was able to speak, she told her father. Unfortunately, by the time he ran back, the man had dropped the papers and had gotten away. She never heard from him or saw him again, but that ordeal impressed in my mother that God would take care of her no matter what she had to go through. In later years, when she was left alone in Africa to raise her three children as a young single mother, she always told us that we were not to worry because God would take care of us. And, he did!

CALL FROM GOD TO BECOME A MISSIONARY:

Catherine had been very active in her church youth group. At one of the meetings after a missionary had been visiting and sharing with the group, she felt the call of God on her life to become a missionary. Unfortunately, not long after this meeting when she was fourteen, the Lord took my grandfather home to be with him. She felt the pressure to leave school and to get a job to help support the family. The dream of going to the mission field was put on the back burner.

England 1934–1955

"The righteous cry, and the Lord heareth, and delivereth them out of all their troubles." Psalm 34:17 (KJV)

After my grandfather passed away, Catherine went to work in a clothing factory and started an apprenticeship to learn how to make men's suits. She continued to go to church but was not too involved in church ministry. After several years of doing this, she decided to train to become a nurse at a local hospital. She was a working girl searching for meaning in her life.

The Courtship:

One day, when she was eighteen, Catherine was walking in the park with her girlfriend and they were introduced to some young men. One of the men she met was a handsome, tall, black-haired, blue-eyed man named Vernon Ranald Riddell, who was known as Ron. She was attracted to him. He showered her with attention and they started dating.

Ron's family was from Scotland and he was raised in a wealthy family. He was the last in line of the Ranald clan. My brother's son, Ronald, now holds the title from the Ranald clan. Catherine found out that Ron did not really have a good relationship with his mother so he had left home to join the army. Catherine was swept off her feet by this Scottish suitor, fell madly in love with him and so began their courtship.

In 1939, Ron was about to be shipped out to fight in the Second World War. These young lovers decided to get married. Catherine describes the first time Ron took her home to Scotland to meet his parents as a disaster!

Catherine was from Yorkshire and it was the custom of people from that area to call everyone "love." They would use this term with everyone they met and it did not have anything to do with relationships. For example, when ordering fish and chips (which to the British is like the Americans ordering hamburgers), she would say, "May I have an order of fish and chips, love?" or when saying thank you after receiving her order she would say "Thank you, love."

Catherine and her family did not own a car and they rode the bus. Although they were not extremely poor, they were working class people. They did not use fancy language or put on airs, have servants or speak the proper Queen's English. My father did not prepare her for meeting his high class family!

My grandmother Riddell was not pleased with my father's choice of a bride. She thought my mother was of a lower class of people. She was dismayed when she heard my mother using the word "love" when addressing complete strangers. She complained to my father that she was a flirt and not to be trusted around other men! My father thought it was amusing, but Catherine cringed at the reception she received. I remember that even as children, we felt like we were not good enough. Whenever we visited them as a family, we had to sit quietly and not be heard. We had to keep our socks and shoes on and always be dressed up. If we visited my other grandmother, we could play in the sand box, sit on the steps and eat jam sandwiches, laugh and be ourselves.

When my parents went to fill out all of the papers you needed to complete in those days to be married, Ron was shocked to find out a secret he had never been told. He had been adopted in Africa and was not his parents' biological child. Later on, my grandmother got angry, she blurted out the following story to Catherine but swore her to secrecy since she said my grandfather would be furious if the story ever got out.

A SORDID PAST:

They say we all have skeletons in our closets and this certainly was one for our family. My grandfather had gone to Africa when he was just a child. His parents were Scottish. When he finished his schooling, he started working in Africa on the police force and he became a lead detective. He met my grandmother who came from a wealthy family and who had been born and raised in Rhodesia, Africa. They got engaged to be married, but just before the wedding, my grandfather had an affair and his mistress had gotten pregnant. He had wanted to be released from his engagement to my grandmother. She refused to free him from his pledge of marriage which would have brought on a scandal in the family and in the high class circles in which they lived. They did get married, and they adopted my grandfather's illegitimate child.

While working as a detective, one of his assignments was to search for and arrest a witch doctor for taking innocent young girls, killing them, and offering them up as sacrifices. The witch doctor was sentenced to death. As his sentence was carried out, he turned to my grandfather and put a curse on him. He said, "For this, you will never be able to rest but you will wander around and not have peace in your life."

Blessings and curses are spoken about in the Bible. We need to have the Holy Spirit reside in our lives so curses cannot take a hold in us. My grandfather was not an active Christian at this time and so this curse became a reality. Throughout his life, no matter where he went, he felt uneasiness. Later on in his life, he had to have a metal plate put in his head for some disorder and he was easily upset. Once you have the Holy Spirit living in you, there is no room for an evil spirit to dwell there and curses can be broken. Satan is powerful but God is more powerful and deliverance is possible to those who ask for it.

Ron did not get on well with his mother. When he graduated from school, he and a friend left Africa and went to England where they joined the army. After Ron left Africa, his parents returned to Scotland. Because of the metal plate in my grandfather's head, he was unable to tolerate the hot weather. They had never told Ron about his birth. No wonder the relationship between the mother and son had been strained from the beginning!

Married Life Begins:

Although his mother did not approve of Catherine, my parents were married in England in 1939 when Catherine was nineteen. Ron went to war and Catherine, who did not want to be a war-time nurse, became an ambulance driver. God protected them both through the many dangerous situations they experienced during the war and they were thankful for that.

Ron was a tanker but also did some undercover work for the army. Ron worked under General Erskine who was a well-known general in the British army. He was part of the Desert Rats and was a fearless soldier. Catherine found out in later years that he had a temper and would have been promoted to a higher position if he had learned to control it! After he became an active Christian, God changed him and at the end of his life, he was a man full of patience and zeal for his Lord.

Disappointments Can Lead to God's Appointments:

Because of the war, their first child was not born until December 1944. My brother, Charles, was the joy of their lives. However, Ron was still living in the barracks at this time and would only come home when he got time off. The separation was hard on their marriage. It was during this time that Catherine found out some awful news— Ron was having an affair with another woman!

Sometimes, our greatest disappointments in life can lead us to God's appointments. For Catherine, this was a turning point in her life. When she met Ron, she had fallen in love with him but had not really made it a matter of prayer before getting married to him. Although he was a good man, he was unchurched and did not know Jesus Christ as his personal savior. He had started to go to church with her but was not a committed Christian at this time. Catherine also did not consider the fact that she had felt the calling of God in her life to become a missionary.

The Bible teaches us in 2 Corinthians 6:14:

"Be ye not unequally yoked together with unbelievers; for what fellowship hath righteousness with unrighteousness? And what communion hath light with darkness?" 2 Corinthians 6:14 (KJV)

The Bible tells us that we all need to make a choice to accept Christ in our lives and have a personal relationship with him. God sent Jesus to this earth to pay for our sins because he loves us so much, and he wants to spend eternity with each one of us. The problem is that God is a Holy God. Those with sin cannot inherit heaven and have eternal life.

You may consider yourself an upright person and not a sinner. But this is what the Bible says about mankind,

"For all have sinned, and come short of the glory of God." Romans 3:23 (KJV)

"For the wages of sin is death; but the gift of God is eternal life through Jesus Christ our Lord." Romans 6:23 (KJV)

I love the fact that God our heavenly Father loves us so much. He knew we had nothing in us that could pay for our sins and allow us to go to heaven. No matter how good we may think we are, we can never be holy enough to enter heaven on our own merit. That is why God made a plan for us and he put this next verse in the Bible,

"For God so loved the world, that he gave his only begotten Son, that whosoever believeth in him should not perish, but have everlasting life." John 3:16 (KJV)

It is so good to know that we do not have to be perfect or try to win God's approval on our own merits. We just have to come to God, confess our sins and ask him to forgive us. Then, we can accept his wonderful gift of eternal life. Once we do this, we never have to worry about our future or what will happen when we die.

We have a wonderful future ahead. We are going to spend eternity, which is forever and ever, with God in heaven. It is such a glorious place that our language cannot adequately express all we will possess one day. In exchange for this wonderful gift of eternal life, God wants us to love him and fellowship with him on a daily basis. Loving God and spending time with him is the reason why he created us. Developing a personal relationship with God is a wonderful thing.

Having a relationship with God is not the same thing as having religion and obeying strict rules. It is enjoying life to the full and having a heart full of joy and peace.

If you have not made this decision yet in your life, you do not need to wait until you go to church or speak to a minister about it. Right now you can accept Christ into your heart and have him become your Savior.

"If we confess our sins, he is faithful and just to forgive us our sins, and to cleanse us from all unrighteousness." 1John 1:9 (KJV)

Catherine confessed her mistakes to God and asked him to save her husband and to restore their marriage. She was able to forgive Ron and through this incident, my father became a true born again Christian. From that time on, they had a Christian marriage. The words to a familiar song "each for the other and both for the Lord" happened to them.

GOD HEARS A CHILD'S PRAYER:

In 1947, Catherine once again became pregnant. My brother decided he wanted two babies from the Lord. Every night he would pray that God would send him two babies. Catherine kept on telling him that God was going to send him one baby, but he insisted he wanted two babies. She tried to tell him he was only going to get either a baby brother or a sister. She knew how disappointed he would be when only one baby was born. Her pregnancy went well but she had gained more weight than she had with my brother. It seemed like she was having more movement, but the doctor insisted she was only having one baby.

Two weeks before our birth, the doctor told her she was indeed having twins. Whenever we irritated my brother as we were growing up, we would remind him that he was the one that prayed for the two of us; so, it was his fault he had to contend with two sisters at the same time.

GOD IS CONCERNED WITH THE DETAILS:

When Ron got out of the army, the Lord blessed him with his own garage. He was a mechanic and God prospered his business. But, he always had a desire to go back to Africa where he had been born and search for his biological mother. Catherine had no desire at that time to leave her mother and go to Africa with three small children. They prayed about it and she told Ron that if God wanted us there, he would need to do three things for us as a family. First, he would provide a job for Ron. Second, he would provide housing for us. Third, he would provide the means so the whole family could go over there together at the same time. She thought she was quite safe. She felt that God would not do these impossible things for them and they could continue their lives in England.

I think Catherine forgot what she learned as a child and that is nothing is impossible for God to do for us if we only believe.

"And to the angel of the church in Philadelphia write; These things saith he that is holy, he that is true, he that hath the key of David, he that openeth, and no man shutteth; and shutteth, and no man openeth." Revelation 3:7 (KJV)

Once again, God did a miracle. God opened what seemed like an impossible door to be opened. Ron was offered a good paying job at a garage in Umtali, Rhodesia. It not only had a good salary but housing to go along with it. The family could stay together and all go at the same time.

So in 1955, Ron and Catherine and their family took a huge step of faith. They said good-bye to friends and family in England and boarded an ocean liner and moved to Africa. They did not know what was ahead for us but knew God had a plan and they could trust him.

AFRICA 1956–1958

"For I know the thoughts that I think toward you, saith the Lord, thoughts of peace, and not of evil, to give you an expected end." Jeremiah 29:11 (KJV)

The trip over to Africa took two weeks. It was a wonderful two weeks of unaccustomed luxury. The meals were delicious. They had activities planned for every age group. When we crossed the imaginary line of the equator, there was a big ceremony and party. The people on board were friendly and the staff were courteous.

The closer we got to Africa, the warmer the weather became. The ship had two holding areas that they made into swimming pools. There were two missionaries on board that took an interest in us and taught us how to swim. It was a time of relaxation and fun for the whole family.

We stopped at different ports and experienced things we had never seen before. At the Madeira Islands, the waters were bright blue and clear. Men would dive for change thrown overboard to them. At each port, there would be people selling their wares. It was indeed a time for us to see many different nationalities that we had never seen before. We had lived a very sheltered life in England and we were only used to seeing white people.

We arrived in Cape Town to an unaccustomed sight. When we got off the ship, we saw rickshaw boys with their homemade carriages. These men had their faces painted and were dressed in bright-colored outfits made out of beads. Their headdresses and outfits resembled the outfits worn by the North American Indians of the Wild West. These carts were built like an open carriage with two large wheels and had handles like a wheelbarrow. They were painted in bright colors. The men would hold on to the long handles and, leaping into the air, they would take off with their passengers. For a fee, they would take daring passengers for a ride along the streets by the docks. It was something new and exciting and, much to our delight, we all went on one of these rides.

There were also women sitting on the ground, weaving baskets and displaying items they had crocheted. There were men who had carved out wooden animals and made items out of soapstone. They were all trying to sell their wares to earn money to provide for their families.

We got on a train that would take us north to our new home in Umtali, Rhodesia. It took several days to get to Umtali. The train would stop every now and then to let off passengers and pick up new ones. Wherever we stopped, we would see Africans on the side of the railroad tracks begging for money. We had never seen such poverty before. In the distance, we could see mud huts with thatched roofs where the Africans lived and we wondered if that is what our house was going to look like.

We eventually arrived at our destination, and we were taken to a hotel where we stayed for a week until our belongings arrived and we could move into the apartment that had been assigned to us.

A New Life Begins for us in Umtali, Rhodesia:

Ron started his new job. We found a small church to attend and schools to go to. Everyone seemed friendly and we soon settled in. Catherine would get up every morning and declare what a beautiful day it was. She was used to English weather where it rained a lot and you got snow in the winter. Here, we were living in the tropics and every day was warm and sunny. Even in the rainy season, it would rain and then an hour afterwards, the sun would come out again. My parents started helping in the little church where we attended, teaching and using their gifts for the Lord. The congregation became like family.

My parents were able to buy a house in a nice district for us to move into. We had fruit trees and fresh vegetables growing in our own garden. We felt like millionaires! Life was good and we were happy!

The Beginning of Sorrows:

At the beginning of 1958, Ron got a lump on one of his fingers. Since it was getting larger, the doctor said he needed to have the lump removed, which was done. However, the lump grew back again, further down on his finger. This time he needed to have his finger amputated.

Although this was a traumatic experience for my parents, as children, we did not realize the severity of such an operation. Ron always had a good sense of humor and he tried to put us at ease. I remember going with my mother to the hospital to see him after his operation. He asked if we wanted to see his finger. He handed us a brown paper bag which he said contained his finger. Catherine scolded him and told him he should not do such a thing! However, he laughed at her. We gingerly opened up the bag only to find he had placed a carrot inside, much to my mother's relief.

Ron came out of the hospital but instead of feeling better; he started having more pains in his body and after several months, was unable to work. For nine months, he was in and out of hospital. The doctors were stumped to know what was wrong with him. He was treated for thrombosis in his legs and given blood transfusions. He was treated for infectious diseases but to no avail. He had been a big man but was losing weight and could not keep food down. They were giving him morphine for the pain; which at first gave him some relief; but, by the end of his life, it was not adequate to keep the pain away.

One day, Catherine was lying on the bed next to him and she had a dream. She saw herself on the top of a mountain. She was trying to hang on to the peak of the mountain, but she began to panic as she felt her hands losing their grip and she started falling. All of a sudden, she found herself safe on the ground at the bottom of the mountain. She heard a voice saying, "I will never leave you or forsake you," and then she woke up. She was telling Ron about her dream and he said to her, "Cath, that voice was the Lord. I have been asking God how I could leave you here in Africa to raise our three children all alone, but now God has given me peace. I know that he will take care of you."

The next day Ron went to be with the Lord. After he died, they did an autopsy to determine the cause of death. They found that he had pancreatic cancer and that the cancer was as big as a large grapefruit. In those days, they didn't know how to x-ray the pancreas and so had not diagnosed his condition. He was forty-one years old and Catherine was only thirty-nine. Overnight, she went from being a loving wife and attentive mother of three young children to a being a widow and a single mother, living in a foreign land very far away from her family in England.

OUR STEPS ARE ORDERED BY THE LORD:

At first, Catherine was not ready to accept the fact that Ron was gone from this life. At his funeral, she fully expected to see a miracle and God would raise him from the dead. At the grave site, she kept on saying to God, "When are you going to do this miracle, Lord?" When it did not happen, she was so angry at God. She had not grieved because she thought this miracle was going to take place and she felt that God had made a fool out of her.

One day, our missionary friend, Pastor Flewelling, came around to visit her and he gave her some godly counsel. He told her a true story about a woman who had a son who was a wonderful Christian young man and youth leader in his church. One day, he got an illness and he died. The mother was so angry with God. She took hold of her son's shoulders and she looked up to heaven and said to God, "Your word says that whatever we ask in your name, you will give to us. It says that by your stripes we are healed. So, if you don't give my son back to me, you are a liar!" This was blasphemy but God instead of striking her down gave her what she demanded. Life came back into her son's body. He turned to his mother and asked her why she had done that because he had been in such a wonderful place and did not want to come back to this earth. The boy recovered. Years later, he committed a murder and was sentenced to die for his crime. He may have repented before he died but what a sad ending to his life all because his mother demanded what she thought were her rights.

The pastor told Catherine that God knows what is best for each of our lives. He knew what was ahead for this young man. He took him to heaven while he was in a place of working and loving God with all his heart, leaving behind a great testimony. God knew there was something down the road this man was not going to handle. So in his mercy, he took him home to heaven while he was in a good place in his life.

Pastor Flewelling said that God knew what was ahead in Ron's life and that we are not to question God and demand him to do things our way. He said when we do this, then we are trying to manipulate God. We have to accept from God's hand what he knows is best for us.

"For my thoughts are not your thoughts, neither are your ways my ways, saith the Lord." Isaiah 33:8 (KJV)

The verse at the beginning of this chapter stated that God has a plan for each of our lives. While we are going through the struggles we experience in life, we cannot always see the good; however, looking back, we can testify that through it all God never left us and he never will.

"Let your conversation be without covetousness; and be content with such things as ye have: for he hath said, I will never leave them nor forsake thee." Hebrews 13:5 (KJV)

The Bible teaches us that there are seasons that we go through in life. No one goes through life on a high all the time. Without seasons of testing, we would not grow in God because we would feel we could handle everything on our own. The hard seasons in life help us to turn over the reins of our lives to God. Our job is to go to God and ask him to help us and change us to be more like him.

We are to trust God in the good seasons and the bad seasons in life. We are to believe that even when we go through trials, difficulties, loss, and sadness, he is there all the time. If we will allow him to change us and mold us through the difficult seasons in life, we will become useful to God.

Isaiah 46:4 is one of my favorite verses in the Bible and it says: "And even to your old age I am he; and even to hoar hairs will I carry you: I have made, and I will bear: even I will carry, and will deliver you." Isaiah 46:4 (KJV)

Catherine repented of her anger toward God. She thanked God for his promise to her that he would be with her throughout her lifetime and that he would never leave her or forsake her. She made a decision to stay in Africa because she had fallen in love with the country and did not wish to return to England.

Africa 1959–1964

"Trust in the Lord, and do good; so shalt thou dwell in the land, and verily thou shalt be fed.

Delight thyself also in the Lord; and he shall give thee the desires of thine heart.

Commit thy way unto the Lord; trust also in him; and he shall bring it to pass.

And he shall bring forth thy righteousness as the light, and thy judgment as the noonday."

Psalm 37:3-6 (KJV)

The next six and a half years, Catherine said she learned to know God in a personal way. She not only had head knowledge about God but he became her friend. She desperately needed him to give her strength, guidance and protection, and to be her provider.

Catherine was a giver and she would reach out to bless others all the time. I remember asking her why she always wore the same dress to church on Sundays. She told us that she wore it because she liked it so much. She would buy material and make my sister and me new dresses for special occasions and make sure Charles had nice clothes to wear. Only in later years did I understand that her motto was "Jesus first, others next, and yourself last." She really believed this saying and lived by it. She never complained about her needs and did not ask for handouts. She put her trust in the Lord and he supplied our needs.

She believed God for our protection also. Many times we would hear the Africans rioting. Our house was the first house on the river that they would come to. As a child, I would be so afraid that they would attack and kill us, but my mother was brave and trusted God for our protection. He never let us down.

She got a job as a receptionist in a lawyer's office where she answered the switchboard and did some office work. The job did not pay a lot of money. However, Catherine always reminded in us that God would take care of us and we had nothing to worry about. My brother, who was fourteen when my dad died, wanted to help support the family. So, as soon as he was old enough, he took his school leavers examination and passed it. He got a job with a telephone company and was trained to be a telephone engineer. Once he was earning some money, he would give Heather and me some pocket money as well as help my mother with the monthly bills. It is always nice to have a big brother, and I thank God for him.

GOD CONTINUES TO DO MIRACLES FOR US:

"But my God shall supply all you need according to his riches in glory by Christ Jesus." Philippians 4:19 (KJV)

One memory I have of this time, when our income was so limited, is the day my mom told us that we needed to pray and ask God to send us some meat and that we should ask him for a roast. She had set the table for supper when we heard a knock on the door. She went to answer it and a man from the church was standing there. He said, "Mrs. Riddell, we had these extra potatoes and I thought maybe you could use them." Catherine thanked him and brought in the potatoes. On the top of the sack, there lay a large roast beef. God is so good!

HEATHER'S MIRACULOUS HEALING:

For some time, my twin sister Heather had been having shortness of breath. Many times her lips would turn blue and we would find her passed out. My mother had told us never to roughhouse with her because of this condition. The doctor had told Catherine that Heather had a hole in her heart and that she would need an operation to try to correct the problem. However, Catherine would have to take her back to England because they did not do this operation in Rhodesia at that time. He told Catherine that there was a fifty percent chance of the surgery being successful but that Heather could die on the operating table. When she was twelve years old, these attacks were becoming more frequent. Catherine made arrangements to take Heather to England for this operation. Friends were willing to take care of Charles and me while they were away. It was a frightening thing to face, but the doctor said Heather was going to definitely die if they did not take this risk.

A week before they were to leave to go to England, an evangelist from Canada came to hold meetings in our town. His name was Reverend Lorne Fox. He was an accomplished pianist. He would put on a short concert, preach and then pray for the sick. When we got to the meeting, everyone was told that if they wanted prayer for healing to fill out a card with their need written on it. At the end of the service, they would be called up to the front where they would receive prayer.

Catherine filled out a card for Heather, and at the end of the meeting Heather went up to wait in the line to receive prayer. As she was standing there, she felt one of her attacks starting. She prayed that she would not have an attack and embarrass herself in front of everyone. Suddenly, the minister left the beginning of the line and came to where she was standing. He took her card and read it out aloud to the congregation. He told them, "There is a little girl here with a hole in her heart. I don't think God wants her to go through life with this condition. I want everyone to stop praying for whatever you are praying for and concentrate on this child. Ask God to give her a new heart." Everyone started to pray for her. She fell over and was lying on the floor. Our pastor saw the left side of her chest rise up and then collapse. Knowing her condition, he thought she had died. However, at the same time the evangelist said, "You can now stop praying and start praising God for this child has a new heart." He then went back to the beginning of the line and continued praying for the other people that needed prayer.

Meanwhile, Heather had come around and was sitting up. Crying and then laughing. When she was able to, she told us what she had felt. She said she had not wanted to make a scene. She was asking God to wait until she got home before she had an attack. She felt this warm sensation came throughout her body like someone put their arms around her and turned on a switch. For the first time in her life, she felt like she could take a huge big breath and that she was walking on air.

When she got home, she wanted a pillow fight with me. She had so much energy. The next day, people at Catherine's work told her to be careful. They said this improvement might only last for a while and that Catherine should still go ahead with the operation. Catherine told them she would prove to them that God had healed her daughter. She took Heather back to the doctors where all x-rays and tests proved to everyone that indeed she was healed. The doctor said she had a brand new heart. She never again had problems with her heart and she never went to England for that operation. She grew up to get married and have three healthy children. We all declared how great our God is!

Although we didn't grow up in our father's presence, my mother made sure our home was a happy home. She had a sanguine nature and would always be willing to do things on the spur of the moment to put a smile on someone's face. She gave us birthday and Christmas parties and we received presents. She loved to decorate our home with homemade streamers and decorations. We always had a Christmas tree full of ornaments. As we got older, if we did not include her in all of our activities, she never selfishly held us back.

She loved to bake and was known for her famous sausage rolls and apple pies. She encouraged us to bring our friends around to the house. She was well loved by all those who knew her. Our home was always full of laughter.

Catherine had a good sense of humor. Often we would watch the Lucille Ball comedy show, *I Love Lucy*, and we would tell her that she reminded us of Lucy Ball.

One memory I have of her using her whit is when she took us to the store to buy winter coats. We found out that the store was a very expensive store and the lady clerk waiting on us was a snob. She brought out these coats that were too high in price for us to purchase. However, my mother, who did not want to slink out of the store with the disapproving looks of this arrogant clerk, asked the lady if perhaps she didn't have anything that was of a better quality!

When we left the store, we thought we should let my mom know that those coats were of the highest quality. She replied, "Oh, I know, but I wasn't going to let that lady think we were anything less than God's children. She was looking down her nose at us!" We all had a good laugh. God provided us with beautiful coats at the next store that were half the price of the ones in the expensive store. God knows how to take care of his children and we were learning from my mother's example that we were "God's kids."

OUR YOUTH GROUP:

Catherine was also a very wise person. When our little church did not have an active youth group, she allowed us to join another youth group at a Full Gospel Church. This youth group was on fire for God and was led by Pastor and Mrs. Hartley. They had a really good rapport with the young people.

I remember when they were telling us about appropriate dating behavior for Christian youth. Mrs. Hartley said that she had been dating her husband for several months and he had not even asked if he could hold her hand. One night, she wanted him to put his arm around her, so she thought she would drop a subtle hint. She kept on moving a little closer to him declaring that it was a little chilly that evening. He did not take the hint. She snuggled a little closer and gave him another hint. Unfortunately, he did not seem to have a romantic bone in his body. What he did was remove his jacket and told her she could wear it since he did not think it was cold at all!

It was in this church that I experienced being baptized in water and also in the Holy Spirit. It was also during these teenage years that I received the call of God to go into ministry, just like my mother had felt in her teenage years. I do not remember if we were studying about Joan of Arc in school, but I got it in my head that I would be willing to be burned at the stake for my Lord like she was. Years later, I was so glad that the Lord doesn't always answer our prayers, because the thought of being burned at the stake no longer had a great appeal to me anymore. Years later, God did, however, lead me into full-time ministry with my first husband. For over thirty years, we worked together with Teen Challenge and the Bible school associated with this organization until his death in 1998.

GOD CONTINUES TO DO MIRACLES FOR US:

Another miracle that happened during this time is that God saved Catherine from drowning. We would take our vacations at a seaside town called Beira, across the border in Portuguese East Africa. It was a beautiful seaside resort and a favored Rhodesian vacation destination. There were clean camping grounds with bathroom facilities with places you could cook and eat. We would vacation there with other church families and always looked forward to these times.

One day, Catherine was in the water when a strong under current pulled her out to sea. She was shouting for help, but those on the shore thought she was just waving at them. When she thought she was going under for the last time, an uncle recognized she was in trouble. He and my brother used a fishing line to go out into the sea, rescue her and bring her to shore. She had to be given CPR, but they revived her and God saved her so we were not left as orphans.

I am so glad the Lord allowed my mother to live until she was in her eighties. She was such an inspiration to us and teaching us the principles of God. Because of her example of faith and trust in God, all three of her children learned to trust and love God too. Many times throughout my life when I have been faced with difficulties and tests, I have drawn from my mother's courage and life of faith: it has strengthened me to keep trusting God for the answers.

ON THE MOVE AGAIN:

In 1963, Catherine got an opportunity to get a good job on with the railroads. It meant we had to move to a town called Bulawayo. Since it meant quite a big pay increase, she accepted the position and we moved to this town.

When we had our farewell at the church, it was also the welcome party for the church's new pastor and his wife. The people loved my mother and our family and were so sad to see us moving. I believe they gave more attention to us leaving than welcoming the new pastor. Although he did not say anything, I am sure that in his heart he was a little miffed about how everyone was talking about Cath Riddell and not really paying any attention to him. I mention this here; because, in a later chapter, you will see how God changed his heart about my mother!

GOD GAVE MY MOTHER ANOTHER DREAM:

One night after we had left Umtali, Catherine had a strange dream. She dreamed that she was climbing in bed with a black man. She curled up in bed with him and he had his arms around her. She felt so secure, contented and loved. She then woke up. She did not think much about this dream until the following year. God then showed her the meaning of this dream and he showed her his plan for the next part of her life.

In the beginning of this chapter we used verses in Proverbs 37 that declare that if we put our trust in God and serve him, he will give us the desires of our hearts. My mother was faithful in trusting God. She was soon to find out that our God is a God of second chances and he was about to reward her with the desires of her heart.

EDMUND COOKSEY

"For the gifts and calling of God are without repentance." Romans 11:29 (KJV)

Edmund Cooksey was born in Yorkshire, England, not far from where my mother was born and raised. He asked Jesus Christ to become his Savior at the age of thirteen. From that early age, he loved to be involved working in the church, doing evangelism work, and later doing some preaching.

He felt that he was called to give his life to God and planned on becoming a preacher or a missionary. He decided to make plans to go to seminary after high school. One day, his friend invited him to go to a service where a Pastor Stephen Jefferies, a famous worldwide evangelist, was holding meetings in the nearby town of Wakefield.

Pastor Jefferies began to preach and Ed was not at all impressed with him. His English was not very good. He whispered to his friend, "I thought you said this man was a good preacher. Why he can't even speak English correctly." His friend whispered back, "Just wait awhile," which he did. After a while, Ed was gripped by the power of his message and by three words which he used repeatedly, "You religious hypocrites." Each time he said these words, it seemed as if he was pointing right at Ed.

God spoke to Ed's heart and that afternoon, he realized that he was a professing Christian but he did not really know Christ in a personal way nor was the love of God being demonstrated in his life. He returned for the evening service. After the pastor finished preaching, he saw things he had never seen before. He saw miracles—blind eyes being opened and those who could not walk getting out of their wheelchairs.

Ed desired to be used of God in this way. He was no longer happy to just attend a service and give a lesson. He wanted the power of God to be demonstrated with signs following the preaching of the word.

COLLEGE DAYS:

After high school, Ed went to the University of Birmingham where he graduated with a teaching degree. During his years as a full time student, he attended the Assemblies of God Church and he grew in his Christian walk. He became very active in Christian work, walking six miles each way to get to church and attending services on Sundays as well as Tuesdays and Saturday evenings. He said these were wonderful years. Toward the end of his university career, God began to speak to him about going to Africa as a missionary.

One day he saw a big notice in the main entrance lobby of the university: "Wanted in Rhodesia, a qualified teacher." These words seem to leap from the notice board and burn themselves into his mind. On that day, he could not concentrate on the lectures because he knew that God had called him to Rhodesia. The call of God was so strong in his life that just before he was due to write his final exams for his degree, he was prepared to quit the university and enroll in the Assemblies of God Bible School in London. In fact, he was on his way out to mail the application for this purpose.

As he was about to open the door, however, a letter fell from the letter box. The letter was from his brother. It read, "I don't know why I must write to you like this, but I feel God would have me tell you to beware of making the same mistake that Moses made of moving too soon and hindering the plan of God." This spoke to Ed, and he never mailed his application. He completed his university course, took his degree in education and started teaching in the city of Birmingham.

MARRIED LIFE:

For the next seven years, he taught and had an active ministry preaching in different churches. God blessed his ministry but his life was not absolutely content. In 1934, he met and married his first wife. Shortly after the marriage, they read the following advertisement in the *Redemption Tidings*, the official publication of the Assemblies of God: Wanted in Rhodesia: Qualified Teachers to Serve as Missionaries. It was almost the identical words that Ed had seen on the notice board in the university many years ago. God spoke to his heart to go. However, since they had just recently been married, they thought they should get adjusted to the marriage before taking on such an assignment. They ignored the call. The next four years were unhappy for Ed because he knew that he had failed to obey God's leading. In 1937, the same notice appeared and this time they decided to respond.

ACCEPTING THE CALL TO GO TO AFRICA:

Two weeks after they accepted the call to go to Africa in 1937, Ed's father suddenly died, collapsing on the street on his way to a business meeting. His sister was to be married in two weeks and this was a terrible shock to everyone. People began to criticize Ed. They said he should not think of going to Africa now and leaving his mother at such a time. Ed did not want to leave his mother alone, but the call of God was so strong in his life that he had to obey him.

To make matters worse, in October of that year, his wife fell down fourteen steps and badly hurt her kidneys. She was carrying their first child. She was rushed to the hospital where she lay unconscious for the whole weekend. For two nights, Ed called on the telephone every hour to find out how she was doing. Thank God, on the Monday afternoon, their daughter was born, a little mite of three pounds and thirteen ounces. The hospital authorities said she would not live through the night and asked Ed to give her a name. They named the child Sheila. When Ed got home that night, he told the Lord, "If you give this child to me and let her live, I will give her to you as long as she lives." Not only did Sheila live but she grew up to marry a minister and work for the Lord in South Africa.

After this event, people began to taunt Ed and tell him that he was a cruel father for planning on taking such a small child to a country which was riddled with malaria. Back then, people had the idea that Africa was filled with tropical diseases. They also thought that on every corner, you would meet up with a lion or another wild animal.

Ed and his wife started praying for God's direction. They did not know if it was the devil trying to stop them going to Africa or if it was the Lord telling them to wait. One night, a visiting missionary came to their house to eat. In the middle of the meal, she suddenly turned and said, "Edmund, God wants you in Africa." Later that evening as they walked into the church, another person handed him a magazine with an article entitled "The Heart of African Missions." The church secretary gave him a copy of *Redemption Tidings*, which he opened up only to see the same advertisement for a missionary teacher needed in Rhodesia.

A MIRACLE OF FINANCES:

They prayed and decided that it was God who was calling them, but they did not have any money saved. Consequently, Ed would have had to give up his teaching job and go from church to church to try to raise the funds. They decided to ask God to miraculously send the money they needed to pay for their trip to the mission field. Mrs. Cooksey declared she did not know anyone that would give them any money and began to feel depressed about the whole situation. However, when God gives you an assignment, he also provides for you. God spoke to a Christian man in Africa that had done well on the stock market. This man called and told them they did not need to try to raise their own funds for their fares. He was going to pay for their tickets because God had instructed him to do so.

AFRICA AT LAST!

In 1939, they finally set sail for Africa. This was the start of their exciting years as missionaries to Africa.

In 1957, the Lord opened the door for Ed to get his master's degree in African languages. He became proficient in the Bantu and Zulu languages and three other dialects. God used him to translate Bible studies and hymn books into the native languages. He was also able to preach in the native tongues without a translator. They saw many people come to Christ and accept him as their Savior. The Lord blessed their ministry with signs following and many were healed and delivered.

In 1959, Ed was asked to come to America to help with some translations of Bible courses and tracts into the Zulu Soto language. A little old lady came over to him in church and prophesied that he was to go to America, but that he would not stay there. He would return back to Africa someday.

While in America, he became the president of Long Island Bible Institute and also the pastor of the Whiteman Memorial Church. God was blessing their work. But in 1962, Ed felt the call of God to return to Africa just like the little old lady had predicted.

ENDURING MOURNING AND GRIEF:

They returned in 1963. Ed worked as the superintendent of the African work in Umtali. He also became pastor at the little church we had called home for so many years. Not long after taking this position, Ed's wife went to be with the Lord. Ed felt like the world had gone out from under his feet. He was now alone. God's Word says, "I will never leave you or forsake you." He already had a great plan for Ed's life and would continue to use him for his glory.

1964–1966

> "Therefore the redeemed of the Lord shall return, and come with singing unto Zion: and everlasting joy shall be upon their head: they shall obtain gladness and joy; and sorrow and mourning shall flee away."
>
> Isaiah 51:11 (KJV)

Catherine had been a widow for six years. All her children had become teenagers and they had busy lives of their own. My brother had taken a job away from home, and Heather and I were busy with school, sports, and youth group activities. We also had boyfriends to take up our time. Although we were still a happy family, it was a lonely time for our mother.

THE END OF MOURNING AND GRIEF:

It was in 1964 that friends from Umtali invited Catherine to come for a weekend visit. She had wanted to go home to Umtali and put flowers on Ron's grave. It would have been their twenty-fifth wedding anniversary had he lived.

She accepted the invitation and was looking forward to the break. She took the train to her destination. On the Saturday evening, she attended a home group where she was asked to sing a special.

Everyone had been telling her about their pastor, whom they had learned to love. Her friends were trying to play "cupid" and put the two of them together. From memories of our farewell party when she had met him, Catherine had thought he looked very stern and he did not really appeal to her. He, on the other hand, remembered how this "Sister Riddell and her family" had stolen the limelight at his welcoming party, so he wasn't too impressed at the mention of her name either.

Edmund could play the piano. When it was time for Catherine to sing and there was no one to play the music for her, he offered to accompany her on the piano. She thanked him and started to sing. Then she got nervous and forgot some of the words to the song, so he joined in with her and sang along to help her out. When the number was finished, Catherine sat down and thought to herself that it was very nice of him to do that!

God spoke to both of them that evening and neither of them got any sleep that night. After wrestling with God all night in prayer, the next morning Ed knew what God wanted him to do.

The next day was Sunday. After the morning service, the couple Catherine was staying with, who had planned to take her to the cemetery so she could put flowers on the grave, made some excuse for not being able to take her. They said that the pastor would like to take her instead as he wanted to put flowers on his wife's grave.

In the cemetery, Ed asked Catherine if she felt God had spoken to her the previous evening and throughout the night. He told her that he had not slept a wink that night and that God had spoken to him. He said that he knew that God was going to bring an end to their loneliness, mourning, and grief and bring new joy and love into their lives. He asked her right then and there in the cemetery to be his wife and Catherine accepted.

Instead of Catherine catching the train home that night, Ed decided he would drive her back to Bulawayo. He wanted to get to know her better. He had heard all these wonderful reports about her but really did not know her personally. They had agreed to get married because God had spoken to both of them to do so. Now, they were beginning to do what normal people do before marriage, getting to know each other.

On the way home that night, the Lord confirmed to my mother that this marriage was really God's idea and indeed his plan for her life. As they were travelling along and it was beginning to get dark, she turned in her seat to look at Ed. To her surprise, she saw him in silhouette which made him look like he was a black man. She recognized the face as that of the man that she had dreamed of getting into bed with her years ago and how in her dream she had felt so loved and safe. She knew without a doubt that marriage was a God-ordained appointment and that God was directing their steps.

The Wedding:

That evening when Catherine arrived home with Ed, she looked so happy and we knew something was up! When Ed left, we wanted to know all the details. We were so excited for her after hearing her story.

The following months were exciting for Catherine. She was like a teenager again, getting long telephone calls from Ed each evening and visits from him whenever he could get a day off. Every time Ed would come down to see Catherine, he would bring little gifts for her and usually something small for us girls as well. After spending so many meager years stretching her income to raise and bless her children, God had brought someone into her life to spoil her. Ed won my mother's heart and the approval of her children. They were married later in 1964 and God blessed their marriage and their years together in ministry.

God is the God of Second Chances:

Ed encouraged Catherine to be all she could be for the Lord. She loved being a pastor's wife and a missionary. Because of years of ill health, Ed's first wife often had been unable to travel to the different African townships in the bush areas. To get to these churches, they had to travel primitive roads and travelling to get there was rough. Catherine loved to travel and was thrilled to be able to go with her husband and minister along side of him to the people. She loved being a missionary. She felt so fulfilled in this position. She felt God had given her a second chance.

She had not answered the call of God to go to the mission field when she was a younger woman because of family issues. Then, she had met Ron and gotten married and raised a family, but now she had the chance to fulfill her heart's desire and work for the Lord in full-time ministry. Catherine became a wonderful helpmate for Ed and they were so happy together.

She loved every part of the ministry, especially working with the African women and children. She had great empathy for them. The life of the Africans, especially for the women and children, was hard. When they became Christians, their faces would shine and they would wear big smiles and be so grateful to God for saving them. I never heard them complain about their heavy loads, but I heard a lot of praise coming from them when we attended their services.

When we attended the church meetings in their townships, they were always joyful services and the people loved to hear the Word of God being preached. The Africans had great singing voices. Although they did not have musical instruments in these little churches, the people would sing out the hymns and songs they had learned. The music was beautiful as they harmonized and lifted up their voices to God in praise and worship. They truly made a joyful noise unto the Lord.

The men would all sit on one side of the church on wooden benches while the women and children sat on the other side of the aisles. When it was time to pray, they would all close their eyes. They were not conscious of whoever was next to them but they would talk to God out loudly. Only after prayer time was finished could you hear yourself think again!

RETURN TO AMERICA:

In November 1965, Ed received a letter from the United States. It was from Rev. David Wilkerson, founder of Teen Challenge. The opening words of this letter read, "This is an urgent call. Will you accept this challenge?" It was a call to come to direct the proposed Teen Challenge Institute of Missions in Rhinebeck, New York.

Although they hated to leave the ministry that God was blessing in awesome ways, after much prayer, Ed and Catherine knew this was a new assignment from God. In April 1966, they boarded a plane to come to America.

Catherine Smith as a child wearing her Brownie uniform

Catherine and Ron Riddell during their courting days

Mary Riddell, Nellie Smith, Charles
Riddell, grandparents of Caroline

Ron and Catherine Riddell's wedding

The twins, Caroline and Heather Riddell as babies

The Riddell family just before they
left England to go to Africa

Charles, Caroline and Heather Riddell taken on Madeira
Islands, Portugal on the way over to Umtali, Rhodesia

Rev. Edmund Cooksey

Ed and Catherine Cooksey's wedding

Caroline and Heather Riddell just before
they left Africa to come to the USA

Louis and Caroline Correa's courting days

Louis and Caroline Correa's wedding

Harry and Catherine Shumaker's wedding

Jonmark Correa serving in the army in Kuwait

Jason and Renee's Correa's wedding

Marvin Snyder

Marvin and Caroline Snyder's wedding
with Pastor Jerry Helman

Caroline Correa with Ruth Snyder in Israel

Farewell to my beloved twin Heather Coetzee

Farewell to a loving Mom, Margaret Snyder

Farewell to a great brother Jeff Snyder

Jonmark and Shelley Correa's wedding with parents
Barbara and Dick Richter and Caroline and Marvin Snyder

United States of America

"And he said unto them, Go ye into all the world, and preach the gospel to every creature." Mark 16:15 (KJV)

In 1958, David Wilkerson and his wife Gwen were pastoring a church in Phillipsburg, Pennsylvania. David wanted to get closer to God and so had decided to spend a two-hour period of time reading the Word and praying instead of watching television. One night, when his wife was out of town visiting family, he picked up *Life* magazine and saw a drawing of seven young men in New York City who had been arrested for beating to death a handicapped boy in the park. All of a sudden, as he looked at the expressions on the faces of these boys, he started to sob. He felt that God was telling him to go to New York City to try to help these gang members. He was from the country, did not know the first thing about city life, but he knew this desire to help them was from God.

It was hard for anyone to understand why he should have so much empathy for these young killers who had committed such a horrendous crime. All David knew was that God had told him in his spirit that he was to go and try and help them. He told his congregation how he felt.

The people were willing to let him go and they helped pay for his gas to get there. His youth leader accompanied him to the city. They went to the courthouse where these boys were being arraigned.

David interrupted the procedures. He was thrown out of the courthouse and had his photo in the newspapers the next day. Although he was rejected by the general public for trying to help these boys, he was eventually accepted by the gang members. It was through these humble beginnings that the work of Teen Challenge was established. This exciting story is told in detail in the book *The Cross and the Switchblade* by David Wilkerson. God did so many miracles and protected David during those scary days of ministry in the slums of New York.

It was from this work amongst the gangs in Brooklyn, New York that Teen Challenge was birthed. Teen Challenge started out as one residential home designed to help gang-affiliated youth who were drug and alcohol addicted, who wanted to change their lives and surrender to Christ, but had nowhere to go and no one to help them. Through miracle after miracle and with the help of other Christians, a building was purchased and staffed. Today, there are Teen Challenge programs in all major cities throughout the world.

After David established this program, he also realized that these young men needed training. They were all school dropouts. Since they had no schooling, they could not find jobs. He realized they needed to have further biblical teaching to get them grounded as Christians, and they also needed some vocational training so that they could re-enter the world as honest citizens with a future.

A training school was bought out in Rehrersburg, Pennsylvania, where the young men could accomplish these goals. However, some of these Teen Challenge converts had a greater desire to further their biblical studies. They desired to become preachers and/or Teen Challenge staff workers and go back into the streets where they had come from and help rescue other lost youth.

At this time, regular Bible colleges would not accept these young men as students as they did not have their high school diplomas or GEDs. These converts were also from the slum areas and lacked the graces taught in good homes. Many of these unchurched youth were still rough around the edges. They lacked the upbringing of regular college students; however, they had such love for God and for others and zeal to work for God that would put many regular Bible school students to shame.

David felt led of the Lord to open his own Bible school to meet this need and so Teen Challenge Institute of Missions was begun. David Wilkerson and Nicky Cruz drove up to Rhinebeck, New York, to the old Oblensky Estate (part of the John Jacob Astor Estate), walked around the property and proclaimed it for the work of the Lord. John and Carol Kenzy were asked to live at the estate in November of 1965, to set up the curriculum and classes and prepare the way for Edmund and Catherine Cooksey, who would be coming from Africa in the spring of 1966. Edmund Cooksey was the first president of the newly created Bible school and Catherine assisted him as dean of Women and Business Assistant or wherever else she was needed. David Wilkerson had met Edmund

Cooksey during Rev. Cooksey's time in America when he was translating work into the African languages. David knew that Ed was an educator as well as an anointed Bible teacher. God laid it on David's heart to call Ed to prayerfully consider this position.

AMERICA, APRIL 1966:

Heather and I were eighteen years old when our parents accepted the call to come to America. We thought it would be exciting to come with them and check out America. Heather was a trained secretary and shorthand typist. When I graduated high school, I had gone to the Post Office School of Training and was trained in all areas of postal work. My friend and I had also gone to night school and learned bookkeeping and business machines. We felt sure with our training we would be able to get jobs overseas. We all got our passports and green cards and headed off to America for a new adventure.

A NEW AND DIFFERENT LIFE:

I remember reading *The Cross and the Switchblade* on the plane coming over to America. I was eighteen years old but I had led a very sheltered life. I had never heard of drugs like heroin or cocaine, nor knew of anyone who was affiliated with a gang, nor had I heard of a homosexual or met a hippy or an alcoholic. Life in the American culture that I was reading about in this book was foreign to me and we did not know what to expect. We were hoping we were not going to be accosted by someone with a switchblade as soon as we landed in America!

When we got off the plane, David Wilkerson and John Benton, who was the director of the Walter Hoving Home, the rehab center they had opened for women, were there to pick us up. The vehicle they had brought to the airport was a van and Heather and I were sitting several seats back from the front. We kept seeing David turn around to speak with my parents. Since we were used to the driver being on the right hand side of the vehicle in Africa, we thought he was driving and not looking where he was going in all the heavy traffic! It took a while before we realized that John Benton was driving on the left hand side of the car and we could relax.

They took us through the area known as the Bowery in New York City, where you saw people who were drunk just leaning against the walls of buildings or laying on the ground sleeping or passed out. The people were dirty and unkempt. Then, we went through the slums of Brooklyn. As we travelled through these devastated areas, all we saw was poverty, graffiti and broken down buildings with smashed window panes. You sensed a feeling of heaviness and sadness and hopelessness in these areas. We were so glad to find out that we were not going to have to live in the inner city but that the Bible school was situated in upstate New York on a beautiful estate in Rhinebeck, New York.

RHINEBECK, NEW YORK:

We arrived in Rhinebeck that evening and were greeted by John and Carol Kenzy. This young couple had met each other in college in Missouri. As newlyweds, John and Carol arrived at Brooklyn Teen Challenge in June

1964. John served as the director of Education and Evangelism, and Carol served as David Wilkerson's secretary. At an early morning chapel service, David Wilkerson asked John if he would be willing to move to Rhinebeck, New York and set up the new Bible school. The Lord had already spoken to John that this was his calling, so the answer was an immediate yes. The school began with ten students in the fall of 1965. Reverend and Mrs. Cooksey arrived in April of 1966 to assume the position of president of the school. John served as academic dean and registrar.

This forty-four-room Georgian mansion was once the home of Alice and Ivan Oblensky. Alice was the daughter of John Jacob Astor IV, and she and her husband (a Russian prince) lived there sporadically, as they were globe-trotters.

When the property became available at the time of the Oblenskys' divorce, David Wilkerson was able to obtain it through a miracle loan from the Combined Insurance Companies of America, based in Chicago. What an incredible setting for former drug addicts to be welcomed into as they studied the word of God and prepared for ministry. God is truly an awesome God!

Ed was English and from the old school as far as manners and dress was concerned. Since the students were being trained to be men and women of God and ambassadors for him, they were expected to dress and act accordingly. They were not allowed to wear jeans or dress shabbily in class or in chapel services. The men had to cut their hair if it was long and all the clothes the students wore had to be modest, clean and ironed.

After classes in the mornings, everyone had chores and assignments to do to take care of the school buildings. There was the cooking and cleaning to do as they did not have other staff to take care of these things. Good work ethics were taught right along with the scriptures. It was like one big family learning to live and work together.

Heather and I found an apartment in Kingston, across the Hudson River a couple miles away from Rhinebeck. We both got jobs and would come to the school on weekends to visit our parents.

We had to adjust to the American way of speaking as there were many English words that were not the same as what the Americans used. I remember one day after meeting some church folks that one young girl mentioned we were PKs. In England, "PK" was chewing gum and in Africa a "PK" was a bathroom. We thought it very strange that she was calling us these names until we found out that "PK" in America meant Preachers' Kids! The American youth had to adjust to some of our words also. We called the traffic lights "robots" in Africa and the trunk of the car the "boot" and the hood of the car the "bonnet!" We had a lot of laughter trying to figure out some of these words but it did not take long to adjust to our new life and language differences.

ONE VERY SPECIAL STUDENT:

The first day we arrived at the school, I noticed a very handsome young man whose name was Louis Correa. He was one of the students and immediately, we felt a connection to one another.

One of the rules they had at the school was that the students could not date for a year as they were to put all their energies into their studies and the new goals they had set for themselves. Besides that, I was one of the president's daughters and so "off limits" to the students.

Although we were not allowed to date, there were no rules about helping others! Louis was assigned to the kitchen to cook. On my weekend visits, he would ask me to help him in the kitchen and so I did. We got to know each other and we became best friends. We would take long walks around the campus grounds; we would go down to the Hudson River which bordered the property and fish. Although we did not consider this dating, we were spending as much time as we could together and we became the best of friends.

I found out that Louis was born in Arecibo, Puerto Rico, and that he was the second oldest sibling of four born to Francesco and Juanita Correa. His father had been twenty years older than his mother. He had been a sailor and was often gone for long periods of time. He died when Louis was twelve years old and his mother then moved the family to Brooklyn, New York, to be close to her brother and his family. She was hoping to give her children a better life in New York.

Unfortunately, where the Correa family moved in Brooklyn was not a good area. There were gangs and drugs and other vices to contend with. At the age of twelve, Louis started hanging around with friends who were smoking marijuana and drinking. He joined a street gang so he would feel like he belonged. For the next sixteen years, he wandered around in the world of drugs, alcohol, and crime. He spent time in and out of jail and his future looked grim.

"Therefore if any man be in Christ, he is a new creature: old things are passed away; behold all things are become new." 2 Corinthians 5:17 (KJV)

One day, some Teen Challenge converts were witnessing on the streets and they invited Louis to come and see a movie. The movie was about changing their lives and becoming Christians.

Louis sat through the movie and the message really spoke to his heart. At the end, when there was an invitation to come up front and be prayed for, he heard another voice in his head that said, "Get out of here and go and meet your connection because you need a fix." He listened to the second voice and left that store front to go and meet his dealer. That same day the police picked him up and he was taken away to prison.

While serving time in prison, he attended a Sunday service in the chapel. The preacher asked the inmates how many years had they really lived and who were they giving their strength to. The preacher told them not to give their strength to the stranger. When he got back to his cell, he thought to himself, *Up until now, I haven't really been living. I have been giving all my strength and youth to the devil.* The stranger was the devil. He realized that if he kept on living his life the way he was doing, he would either die of a drug overdose or end up serving long years in prison. He didn't want this kind of future for himself.

He remembered the service he had attended in the store front where they had shown the movie of men who had been changed by the power of God. He had heard their testimonies and he sincerely wanted to change. That night he got down on his knees by his bed and asked God to forgive him for his sins. He told God that, if He could change him and use him, he wanted to surrender his whole life to God.

When he was released from prison, instead of going back on the streets, he entered a Teen Challenge program. After three months there, he was sent to the rehab center in Rehrersburg for nine months. He then went on to be one of the first students at Teen Challenge Institute of Missions.

I never knew Louis before his salvation and I was truly innocent and naïve. I had fallen in love with him and could not imagine him being anything but the man of God that he now was. As far as I was concerned, he was a new creature in God and his old life was passed away.

My parents liked Louis. However, like any caring parent, they were able to see some dangers and had concerns about our relationship. Louis has a different nationality and a different culture from mine. He was also thirteen years older than I was. He had been in prison and involved in a life of crime. Not every student with this background stayed faithful to God. Some returned to the life of drugs again. They did not want this for their daughter.

In 1967, I decided that if I was going to be going into ministry with Louis, then I should take some Bible studies myself. I went away to Pennsylvania to a Bible school for a year and took some classes. It was a time that we could pray and make sure that the Lord was in our relationship and wanted us together forever. Our love did not wane. So as time progressed and my parents saw how much we were in love and that keeping us apart was a losing battle, they trusted God to take care of the future. They embraced Louis and welcomed him into the family.

Louis graduated from Bible school in 1968 and we got engaged. He was going to St. Louis to do a three month internship at the Teen Challenge Center there. Then, after our wedding, we were going to return to work with St. Louis Teen Challenge. This was definitely a mission's work. Our housing and meals would be provided but our promised salary was five dollars a week.

When Louis went to Ed to ask for my hand in marriage, Ed asked him how he intended to support me as his wife. The Lord gave Louis great wisdom in his answer. "Brother Cooksey, how can you ask me such a question? You are a man of God, and the same God that has supplied all of your needs is the same God that I serve and I know that he will supply our needs too!" He passed the test with flying colors and so we became engaged.

THE WEDDING:

I had been teaching Sunday school and playing the piano at a small country church at Lomontville, New York. Although it was a small assembly, the pastor and his wife and congregation loved me. We decided that we would get married in that church and then return to the Bible school campus to have an outdoor wedding reception for all of our guests. My mother and Carol Kenzy were the chief bakers and cooks for the affair. Everyone at the school pitched in to put on a wonderful wedding reception for us.

My parents paid for the entire wedding and reception. We went shopping and Heather and I found a beautiful lace wedding dress that we both fell in love with. I wore it and felt like a princess. Later the next year, when Heather got married in Africa, she also wore this beautiful dress. Years later, it was worn by my niece. Although it was expensive, three beautiful brides enjoyed being princess for a day in my wedding dress.

My twin sister, Heather, was my maid of honor and two of my friends from Bible school were my bridesmaids. Renee Kenzy, who was not quite three years old, was my flower girl. She was dressed like a miniature bride and looked adorable.

Louis looked so handsome in his tuxedo. His one brother and my brother and a school friend were the groomsmen. One of our church friends had a little three-year-old that rounded out our bridal party as the ring bearer. At the practice, the two little ones were not performing their tasks very well. My sister bribed them to behave by promising them a bag of sweets (English name for candy) if they walked down the aisle and held hands. As soon as the wedding service was over, Renee was demanding that bag of candy from Heather as her reward for services rendered.

On August 3, 1968, God joined Louis Correa and Caroline Riddell together as man and wife. We honeymooned at Niagara Falls and took our time driving to St. Louis, Missouri. This was to be our first home together and the beginning of thirty years of ministry that God allowed us to share.

1968–1975

Louis had lived in the city all of his adult life and used public transportation. He never learned to drive, nor did he have a father around to teach him anything about cars. I, on the other hand, had never used any kind of public transportation in my life. I didn't know much about cars either, except how to drive them. Heather and I had an older brother who would fix our cars for us and, when he was not around, we would take our cars to the garage.

The first time Louis took Heather and me to Brooklyn, New York, and took us on the subway, we looked around and thought everyone was high on drugs. The lights on the train kept flashing on and off and everyone seemed like they were nodding off to sleep. The train seemed to be going at a tremendous speed. There were clanging and loud hissing noises as it stopped to let people off and others on throughout the journey. Louis played on our ignorance and told us that the people were all either drunk or on drugs and probably carrying hidden weapons. We were quite terrified.

Then, he took us to Greenwich Village and the hippie scene. Again, we thought we had arrived on an alien planet as we could not relate to what we saw in that culture either. Arriving in St Louis and the ghetto that was to become our home for the next year was another culture shock for me.

MARRIED LIFE:

When Louis and I were married, I had to teach him how to drive. I had an old car. As I mentioned before, neither of us knew the first thing about vehicles. Looking back, I can laugh at some of the dilemmas we found ourselves in.

I remember one time the car broke down and we were sitting at the side of the road. Louis opened up the hood of the car and we both stood there staring at the engine. Louis was touching the different cords and wires as if he knew what he was doing. When I asked him about why we were standing there staring at this engine, his reply was, "That is what you are supposed to do when your car breaks down. Everyone opens up the hood and looks at the engine!"

It seemed like every time it rained, our car would quit on us. We found out the noise it made had something to do with the "lifters." We then thought we were really smart because whenever we heard some other car making the same noise, we would say to each other, "Ah, that's their lifters, they need to get them fixed!"

Another time, Louis came into the apartment after telling me the car needed oil and he was going to put it in. He came back some time later frustrated, declaring that there was no way you could get the oil to go into that little hole! I did not know what he was talking about so I headed down to the car. I found out he was trying to put the oil in the hole where the dip stick belonged! We had many laughs after the fact years later when we got a more dependable vehicle and had grown a little in the mechanics of a car. Thank God that he brought men who knew about mechanics around us to assist us with these simple tasks.

St. Louis Teen Challenge:

We arrived in St. Louis for our first ministry job in August 1968. We were put in charge of the new men's home. The ministry had purchased an old house in a poor section of the city. The kitchen, dining room, and chapel were on the first floor; our apartment was on the second floor; the men were housed on the third floor. The director and his family lived across the street in another house that had the office downstairs and living quarters on the second floor.

The men in our home were newly off the streets. Louis was very protective of me and did not want me to become too friendly with any of them. I was from a background where I had many friends, both male and female; we all went to a large youth group and life was simple and trusting. I was very gullible and naïve when it came to the lifestyles from which these men came and I would believe whatever they told me. On the other hand, Louis had much wisdom in dealing with people who had been on drugs, alcohol and in gangs. He was aware of the deception and lifestyles these men were from and so did not trust or believe everything they said or did when they first arrived at the center.

We did see amazing changes in many of their lives as they honestly accepted Christ and gave up the life-controlling habits and exchanged them for true Christian values. However, some did not make it and went back on the streets from which they came. We knew that the seed had been sown and that God would continue to convict and draw them to himself.

GOD'S PROTECTION:

"Because he hath set his love upon me, therefore will I deliver him: I will set him on high, because he hath known my name.

He shall call upon me, and I will answer him I will be with him in trouble: I will deliver him, and honour him."

Psalm 91: 14-15 (KJV)

One of the jobs that Louis and I did was to take a movie called *Youth in a Fix* to the different churches and show it. Louis would then give his testimony of how God brought him out of the lifestyle of sin and into a personal relationship with Jesus Christ. In most churches, we were gladly received and were given an offering for the center, which depended upon freewill offerings in order to function.

One day, coming back from one of these services, it was raining and our car broke down again in the worst area in the city. We were all dressed up in church clothes, carrying this large film. Louis said the car would probably be broken into and he did not want to lose the movie. Louis also had the offering in his pockets. Back then, there were no cell phones. We had to walk through the streets in the pouring rain until we could find a gas station that was open so we could call for help.

I think Louis and I prayed our most powerful prayers for protection that night, walking through the slums and praying we would not be mugged, robbed or raped. Thank the Lord, we did find a garage. Several hours later, we were rescued by the director. We were soaked to the skin and looked bedraggled, but we were safe!

The center had rented a small storehouse shop in the ghetto where they held Sunday morning services. It was called the Gaslight Square District and we were told not to wander the streets alone. Right down from where we held services was a "satanic church," and on the streets you would see prostitutes and unsavory characters hanging out. Sometimes, we would hear a commotion outside the front door during a service, only to find out a fight had broken out or a mugging had occurred.

I helped with children's service as we invited the ghetto children to come to Sunday school or youth club, which we held in the middle of the week. The children responded well, but you never knew when they would come since they did not get much support from their parents who were often involved with drugs. However, we tried to do whatever we were asked to do and we had an earnest desire for God to use us.

One day, we were holding a service when everything began to shake. St. Louis was experiencing a small earthquake. The pictures fell off the walls and a few stones came loose on the outside of the building. Although it was scary at the time, looking back, I have to smile. I remember that most of our congregation ended up at the altar asking God to save them and not leave them behind! There was a lot of confessing of sin that morning!!

Unfortunately when man is confronted with terror, sickness, tragedy or war, the first thing they do is cry out to God for help. When things are going well, they forget about the awesome and wonderful God that loves us and wants a personal relationship with each one of his children. They no longer put him first in their lives.

BIBLE SCHOOL AGAIN:

"In all thy ways acknowledge him, and he will direct thy paths." Proverbs 3:6 (KJV)

In November, I found out that I was pregnant. We were both so happy about the pregnancy. Unfortunately, there was no encouragement for Louis to continue getting his minister's license or ordination. His desire was to become a bona fide preacher. Although we were active in ministry, Louis was only encouraged to give his testimony, because people seemed very interested to hear about that type of lifestyle. Going to the churches to show a movie and give your testimony was how the Center received the finances to exist.

I had never been involved in a lifestyle of drugs and crime. I felt we were being looked at as "second class Christians"—a special brand of Teen Challenge converts. I didn't like that title. We prayed about our feelings and asked God to make a way for Louis to continue his education and realize his dream. After much prayer, we decided that we would look into Louis going back to school to earn his four-year degree in Biblical studies and then apply for his ordination.

My parents at that time were heading up the Long Island Bible Institute and pastoring the church there in Oyster Bay, New York. They encouraged us to join them. We would help them out in the kitchen by cooking the main meal for the students and Louis could finish his schooling. Our car had broken down again. We had invested whatever money we had to try and fix it to no avail. In April 1968, we said goodbye to St. Louis and headed out to Oyster Bay, Long Island, via the plane.

LONG ISLAND BIBLE INSTITUTE, OYSTER BAY:

What a difference in scenery! Gone were the slums with all its poverty and degradation! Oyster Bay was a beautiful village. We could walk down to the park and the Long Island Sound, and spend peaceful times looking out onto the waters surrounding the island. There were places there that we could have barbeques and picnics. We could take walks in the evenings and not worry about our safety. Everyone seemed "normal" and we came to love it there. Louis went to school and we cooked the main meal at the Bible school. We were very happy and content.

APRIL 1969:

The Bible teaches us that life is full of seasons. Sometimes we have a season of great happiness and sometimes we have to experience trials.

A time to be born, and a time to die; a time to plant, and a time to pluck up that which is planted." Ecclesiastes 3:2 (KJV)

Because of our move, I had missed a doctor's appointment. When I went to the new obstetrician, he questioned that I was six months pregnant. I was losing weight instead of gaining and he did not hear the baby's heartbeat. On the fifteenth of April, I went into labor and suffered a miscarriage. We lost our first baby boy. We were very sad.

On top of that, we received more devastating news when I got home from the hospital. On the seventeenth of April, just two days later, we got the news that my mother-in-law had passed away. We went to Brooklyn for the funeral and buried Louis's Mom, then came back to Oyster Bay to continue our lives. We had each other and God comforted our hearts.

Apart from school work and cooking, Louis and I got jobs working the 3–11 shifts in a nursing home as an orderly and nursing assistant. The home was a small Christian home and we enjoyed what we did. We loved the elderly people and it was a nice place to work. I worked on the second floor and Louis worked on the first floor. Whenever I needed help with lifting a patient, I could run downstairs to ask him to help me.

The following year, I got pregnant again and on December 9, 1970, our son Jason Andrew Correa was born. After losing one baby, I was very anxious when the doctor came to me at midnight saying that Jason had a high count of bilirubin in his system and would have to be placed under fluorescent lights. My roommate came back into the room several hours later and informed me that my baby was going to be blind as the little eye mask they placed over his eyes for protection had slipped down over his mouth. She informed me that she thought he was struggling to breathe.

I rushed out of the room to the nursery in a panic only to find out that Jason was fine. The eye covering was just an added precaution and Jason could breathe without any problem. My doctor tried to make light of it telling me that Jason was just enjoying a sun tan and not to worry about him. He told me to get my rest because, once I got the baby home, there would not be much time for that and so I should enjoy it while I could.

After losing one baby, it was easier said than done, and when they told me I would have to leave Jason in the hospital for several days after I was discharged until his levels were within normal values, I was very upset. Louis came to pick me up and accidently drove over the barrier in the parking lot where he was parked and the car was stuck! I was crying and looking out of the window at this fiasco. A couple of men came to Louis's assistance, helped him lift the front of the car up to get the car unstuck so we could leave the hospital to go home!

Jason was released from the hospital a few days later on my birthday, and I became a stay-at-home mother. I so enjoyed my days taking care of my baby and assisting Louis with the cooking and with Bible school activities.

Jason was a happy baby and easy to take care of. He slept well and was fully potty trained at eighteen months of age. It was safe to take him for walks and enjoy the outside activities without fear of being mugged. He had his grandparents and many students around to spoil him.

After graduation, Louis was ordained by the Assemblies of God and we started to minister on the weekends in a little church that did not have a pastor. Under Ed's guidance and mentoring, Louis had grown in his Christian walk. We were so happy and life was good. I am so glad for those years that allowed us to grow and mature in the things of God.

In June 1973, God blessed us with another son, Nigel Paul Correa. Nigel was a delight. Jason was the first baby and so very compliant. Nigel, on the other hand, saw his big brother running around so he was not content to be placed in a play pen. He wanted to copy Jason and do whatever he was doing. He was much more active and kept me on my toes! Our sons brought us much joy and we had a happy family life and ministry that kept us busy and content. Then in 1975, God brought about a change in our lives that we had never contemplated.

GOD SHAKES OUR BOAT:

In 1975, Ed had a stroke and after one week, he passed away. It was a devastating, sad time and my mother decided to go back to Africa to spend some time with Heather. At the funeral, John Kenzy asked Louis if he would consider coming to work at Teen Challenge Institute as the food services director and also help as an instructor.

Although the school was called Teen Challenge, this was a misnomer as all the students were older than eighteen. Many of these young adults stayed at the school in dorms. There were also some who were married with families and they lived in the town of Sunbury and commuted to school.

After our experience in St. Louis, I did not want to go back into Teen Challenge ministry. We had lived for six and a half years at the Long Island Bible Institute. Louis was an ordained minister that was respected as such in the area and I didn't want to go back to being a "Teen Challenge convert" only. We were assured that this would not be the case.

I remember reading about how a mother eagle would make her nest uncomfortable for the baby eaglets to remain there when it's time for them to learn how to fly. The mother bird would get rid of the soft lining of the nest so the twigs would stick out and making the nest uncomfortable for the babies to lie in. She would then nudge the eaglets to the edge of the nest and out of the safe place. They would start to fall and so, in desperation, they would start flapping their wings. The mother eagle would then swoop down underneath the baby eaglets and catch them on her own wings. After doing this several times, the eaglets developed strength in their own wings and soon were flying solo.

So, it is sometimes with us when God has something new for us to do. We would never have left that safe place in Long Island had God not changed our circumstances and made it uncomfortable for us to stay on there. The church was bringing in a new pastor and president at Long Island Bible Institute. We did not feel like we belonged there anymore; so, after much prayer, we knew it was time for us to move on. We accepted this move with much apprehension. We did not understand the importance of this move until years later.

God was going to use Louis's past life history and testimony to win many men to the Lord. He had a good plan ahead for our lives. We just had to trust his leading and take a step of faith.

SUNBURY, PENNSYLVANIA:

We arrived in Pennsylvania over the July 4 weekend. Since our apartment was not ready for us yet and our furniture had not yet arrived, we decided we would camp at a lovely camp area called Knoebels Grove, located just a few miles from the school. Somebody lent us an old tent and, like pioneers of old, we set off with great expectations!

Now you have to remember that Louis was a "city boy" and had never before been camping. We also had two active little boys, a four-and-a-half-year-old and a two-year-old along with us, and we decided it would be fun to try out camping! By the time we managed to get this old tent up (something neither of us had any knowledge of how to do), we were quite exhausted and thought we had accomplished a great feat. Although exhausted, we didn't sleep much that night since our camp site felt more like a rock garden to sleep on and the ground was not very level.

To add insult to injury, the site was the last one next to the road and every time a car came up the road, their headlights would shine directly into our tent. We felt like they were going to run us over. The next morning, we got up to find that most of our neighbors were in motor homes and our tent looked like we were the outhouse! We then found out that we had set up our tent on the wrong site so we had to tear everything down and start afresh on a new site. Thankfully, the next site was in a safer location and it did not take us quite as long to put the tent up because now we had experience from the previous day. Anyway, once we were established, we had a fun time with our children and enjoyed that little vacation before starting our new position at Teen Challenge Institute.

1975–1997

In 1972, a demand note for repayment of the outstanding loan for the property in Rhinebeck, New York, was issued to Teen Challenge. Since they did not have the cash on hand to pay this loan, the Rhinebeck property was put up for sale and the school had to move. Frank Reynolds, director of the Teen Challenge Training Center in Rehrersburg, Pennsylvania, told John Kenzy of the availability of a former Odd Fellows orphanage in Sunbury.

Because the property had been empty anywhere from five and a half to seven years, it was not in good condition, though structurally sound. A caretaker and his wife lived in part of the eighty-two-thousand-square-foot main building, but the rest of the building was unused and neglected. Not only did it need cosmetic work, but the water and sewage systems as well as the heating plant needed renovation. The Education Building was totally non-usable. Two farmhouses on the property were in need of much help. The barn had been partially burned down, but Teen Challenge "inherited" two hundred milk cows with the property which they had to keep for two years.

Other buildings were in disarray and were eventually repaired or removed.

By the time we arrived in 1975, the main building had been renovated with offices in the center building first floor and apartments above on the second floor. To the left and to the right of the center building were the dorm rooms, each with an apartment on the first floor that housed staff. The kitchen and dining room were in the basement on the left side of the building. The sub-basement on the right side of the main building contained an unused old swimming pool where emergency management inventory was stored in case of emergency needs. To the right of the main building was a two-story structure that was called the Education Building. The chapel and library were housed on the second floor. The first floor boasted classrooms and a learning center. The buildings were old but all the rooms had fresh paint and had been fixed up to look decent.

After our short vacation at Knoebels, we got settled into our new apartment. Carol Kenzy helped me wallpaper some of the rooms. Once the furniture arrived and we got settled in, we loved our new home.

We received such a warm welcome from the staff we met, and they shared with us powerful testimonies of what brought them to work with Teen Challenge. Because these testimonies had such an impact on our lives and instilled in us a calling to help people with life controlling problems, I want to share with you a few of these amazing testimonies in this chapter.

When we first arrived, Ron and Martha Perry and their four children were so nice to us. They were in charge of the farm. Their teenage children allowed Jason, who was only four years old at that time, to tag along with them as they helped their parents with the farming duties. Jason, who had been raised in Oyster Bay, Long Island the first four years of his life, loved the country. Shortly after arriving at Sunbury and going to the farm to see the cows, he came running up to me to inform me that the best smell in the whole world was a cow! I tended to disagree with him but he was so thrilled with God's creation and I was so grateful to have such wonderful neighbors that would allow my little boy to experience all these new discoveries. Ron and Martha shared their testimony with us.

Ron had been raised in a dysfunctional family. His father had left and abandoned his family when Ron was only three years old and the family had split up and Ron had gone to live with an aunt where he remained until he was six. His aunt was very good to him and took him to church but unfortunately other uncles abused him both physically and sexually and he was forced to do many duties on the farm that a child his age should not have had to do.

His mother had remarried and when Ron was six years old, his grandmother called her and told her that if she did not come and get her child she didn't think Ron would live much longer. His mother returned for him and he went to live with her and his stepfather when he was six years old.

When he was older, he met his wife. Martha had been raised in a wonderful Christian family and she loved the

Lord. She and Ron fell in love and so they were married and although he had many problems because of the way he had been raised, his wife loved and prayed for him, and at the age of thirty he made a commitment to the Lord. He was a truck driver and he remembers before his salvation one man telling him that he must have a lot of hurt and anger inside of him because he had such a foul mouth. God changed all that.

In 1971, Ron and Martha and their four children came to Teen Challenge Institute to take Bible studies because they felt a call to help people with life-controlling problems. Ron helped with the maintenance and then from 1972–1975, when the school moved to the new property in Sunbury, Pennsylvania, he became a full-time farmer. The farm did very well but because any income it made had to go to supporting the Bible school instead of being reinvested into the farm, there weren't enough funds to keep it running and so at the end of 1975, the dairy herd was sold and the Perry's left the Bible school.

Another staff couple we met were Jerry and Sharon Helman. Jerry was the dean of Education and vice president and his wife was the dean of women. They had a daughter Rachel who was seven.

Jerry came from Michigan. He had one sister who was eighteen months younger than he was. He was raised in a four-room house on his grandparents' property. They were extremely poor. Their house had no running water or indoor plumbing and was heated by a coal stove. Life was hard and they had to walk one-sixth of a mile each way with a bucket in hand to bring water to the house, and they had an outhouse to use for bathroom facilities.

In order to find employment, his father went to Detroit, Michigan, to find work. He did find employment there and moved up in the ranks to eventually become a union representative. Although he had money now, he did not send any money home to support his family.

At first, Jerry's dad came home every weekend but then as time went on, his visits became fewer and fewer until one year, Jerry only saw him about four times that year. His father had been a womanizer and drinker and he had a long-time mistress living with him. Since he did not send support for his family, Jerry was raised in abject poverty which made him feel different from other classmates and he developed a poor self-image and was very shame-based.

Two years after Jerry's graduation from high school, his father left his mistress and begged his wife to take him back. Jerry had a lot of anger toward his dad and for several years refused to communicate with him. However, after his father gave him work at a factory, he moved back home with his parents who now lived next to a Christian family. This family invited him to attend church and about six months later, Jerry accepted Christ in his life as his Savior.

About a year after his salvation experience, Jerry attended a Christ Ambassadors Rally and David Wilkerson was the preacher. What impressed Jerry the most about Dave was that he had kept his commitment to come and preach at this rally even though his own father had passed away that day. David Wilkerson's faithfulness and commitment to preach the Gospel made

Jerry dedicate his own life to Jesus and accept the call of God in his life.

It was a year later, that while attending another camp, he had a vision where he saw the earth rotating around and it was covered by grain. In this vision, he saw people harvesting the grain with sickles and he heard the voice of Jesus say, "I have called you to work for me."

He applied to, and went to North Central Bible College in Minnesota. After Bible school, he pastored a small church in Lake Hubert that was in a very poor area. He stayed there for two years then went back to Michigan and pastored another Assemblies of God church for two years. He then went to Detroit to work in Teen Challenge Center and it was there that he met his wife Sharon.

Sharon used to come to the center on the weekends and help minister on the streets and in the coffee houses. She had a great deal of energy and she had a love for people and the ministry. She was very pretty and Jerry soon fell in love with her.

Sharon was from North Carolina and had moved to Michigan with her father and her three sisters. Her mother had died at the age of forty from uterine cancer and her father was a very controlling man. She had become a Christian as a child and since she was the oldest of the girls, had been responsible to mother her sisters and was in charge of the household at a very young age. She said she had felt the call to ministry since she was a young child.

Jerry and Sharon were married in 1967 and soon became in charge of the women's rehabilitation ministry at Capac, Michigan.

While Sharon had gone into the ministry, her youngest sister Marilyn had gotten involved with drugs and she had also become the mistress to a judge. The Helmans had prayed for her for many years and one day, she had decided she wanted to get her life straight and had made a decision to leave this life of drugs and debauchery behind her. She made the choice to get away from this lifestyle altogether.

However, this is not the easiest thing to do and one night, Jerry and Sharon got the news that Marilyn had been found in her car and she had been shot and killed. This became a cold case and they never found out who killed her, but it gave the Helmans even more incentive to minister to those whose lives had been affected by drugs and dysfunctional lifestyles.

While working in the women's rehabilitation center, they had sent some of their graduates to the Teen Challenge Bible Institute and John Kenzy had heard that Jerry was a good Bible teacher. Jerry and Sharon had the desire to work in the Bible school and eventually in 1971, the Helman family moved to Rhinebeck, New York, to join the school staff. They lived in a small trailer with their three-year-old daughter. It was a little like déjà vu for Jerry, as the first night in Rhinebeck the trailer ran out of heating fuel and it was freezing cold, and the trailer park was full of mud from the rains. They had very little furniture and faced some tough struggles, but Jerry's struggles in his early life had given him an understanding and compassion for people who had been raised in dysfunctional families and in some ways prepared him for his future home missions work.

The Helmans worked at the school until 1983, when they left and became assistant pastors of a small Assemblies of God church in Sunbury, Pennsylvania.

Unbeknownst to us, Sharon had been raped by a man they had been ministering to at Teen Challenge. He was a former student whose mother was a prostitute and he didn't know who his father was. He had been raised without any family values. The Helmans had reached out to help him and he took advantage of the situation and one day raped Sharon. Sharon, like many rape victims, refused to tell anyone of this incident and swore her family to secrecy. Erroneously, she felt that she would be blamed for encouraging this man, and she wanted to just forget the whole thing. This man continued to pursue her and one time, when she was taking Rachel to gymnastics, he showed up by her car again, threatening her. Jerry became very protective of Sharon after these attacks, and this caused them to leave the school in 1983 to pursue pastoral ministry. We were all sad to see them leave.

In 1985, Sharon and Jerry felt a strong urge from the Lord to branch out and start a new church and Brookside Ministries church was founded. Restoration was a main theme for this new church.

The Helmans needed $5,000 in order to pay off all their debts and branch out and start a church. They prayed and wanted God to show them if this was indeed what God wanted them to do at this time. They asked God to supply these funds miraculously and then they would know that this desire was from God. They didn't mention this need to anyone but God.

Shortly after this prayer, a man came to them and gave them an envelope and he told them God had told him to give it to them so they could start the new church. Inside the envelope were fifty one-hundred-dollar bills—the exact amount that they needed. God paid off the debt for them, so they could launch out to start the church.

They had no promised salary but knew that God was in this move and God never failed to supply for them. They called the new church Brookside Ministries Church and it celebrated its twenty-fifth anniversary in 2012. It is a church that is based on the need for people to be restored, and it opens its doors to all those who are hurting in any way and who are seeking for someone to love them. Jesus is the answer and that is what Brookside Ministries Church offers.

In 1985, Sharon was diagnosed with breast cancer. Although she underwent chemotherapy and for a time seemed cancer free, the cancer showed up in her liver. In 1988, the Lord took her home to be with him where I know she received a great reward for her faithfulness to him.

One of the highlights at the beginning of each semester was the new student banquet when the students would give their personal testimonies telling where they were from, how they became Christians, and why they came to the school. The greatest miracle that God can do for us is to transform us from sinners to Christians. He does this when we come to him and ask him to forgive our sins and we turn away from them and we accept his free gift of salvation he offers to us.

Again, I want to share a few of these testimonies because of the impact they had on my life. I hope these true stories will give you a new love for those you may meet along life's way that are hurting, lonely, hopeless and lost. God changed the lives of these students so dramatically and it made me realize that nothing is impossible with God. Man may give up on you but God never does. What he has done for others, he will surely do for all of us who put our trust in him.

Florence Ivery came from Chicago. She had been raised in a single parent home. At age thirteen, she would sneak out of the house after her mother left to work her night shift job. She started smoking marijuana and drinking to be accepted in her peer group. She also started staying away from home for days at a time and then months at a time.

Her mother decided to move from Chicago to California to give them a fresh new start on life. Instead of improving her life, Flo got involved with taking heroin and in order to pay for her habit, she started dealing drugs. At twenty-seven years old, she was arrested and sentenced to a year in the Los Angeles County Jail.

Once she got out, she went right back to selling drugs. Unfortunately, her own habit was growing and so she started stealing and also entered the life of prostitution to make ends meet.

At age thirty-five, she returned to Chicago but continued this lifestyle going in and out of jail. She spent thirty-three years living such a life. Her friends were dying from overdoses of drugs or serving long sentences in prison or worse yet, being murdered by the people they had ripped off for drugs.

One day, a group of Christians moved into the neighborhood and came on the streets to witness to the addicts. After several attempts to witness to Flo, a man named Bob got through to her and she accepted Jesus as her Savior. She went to the induction center they had opened in the neighborhood and two days later, she was on her way to Detroit Teen Challenge.

After she completed that program, she came on to the Bible School in Rhinebeck. She was so thankful for the second chance that God had given to her. Her friend who had been with her that day she went into the Induction Center refused to go with Flo, but instead went off to get high. She was found the next day stabbed to death and thrown out of a three-story building. Flo realized that if it had not been for the grace of God in her life, that could have been her fate.

Robert Monzon was from the Bronx and his drug problem started early. At age thirteen, when he was in junior high school he became involved in the gang life by joining a gang called the Young Sinners. One night, there was a fight between the Imperial Hoods and the Young Sinners. One of the gang members had a gun and when Robert and his friend came across two young men, who they thought to be from the rival gang, his friend asked Robert to give him the gun. Somehow, while passing the gun to his friend, it went off and hit one of these men in the chest. Even though he was only thirteen years old, he was incarcerated and sent to Lincoln Hall, a Catholic school. Here, he met other young men who were sent to the same school because they were involved in similar cases of delinquency, drug addictions and teen alcoholism. Instead of changing for the better, Robert got deeper into drugs and alcohol. When he was released after serving his sentence, he continued his downward spiral, going from detention centers to jails.

When he was seventeen, he was sentenced to three years at Rikers Island Prison. He was considered incorrigible. Prison life was terrible for him. At the induction center, he picked a fight with a man who was giving him suggestive looks, and after the guards stopped the fight, they took him to a back room and beat him into submission. They wanted to show him who was in charge.

Because of his young age and high test scores, after ninety days, they put Robert in a parole program. A couple months later, he was released from prison and went straight into this parole program. Although he was given this opportunity to go straight, he went right back to taking drugs. It was a parole officer who told him about Teen Challenge, but it took twelve years of this lifestyle before he was ready to make a change. Robert went through the induction center in Brooklyn, the rehab center in Rehrersburg and on to the Bible school.

He had always heard that "Once a drug addict, always a drug addict," but he found out with God that does not have to be a fact. Now, he was a brand new man.

He graduated from Bible school, earned his BA, MA, and DD. He and his wife are still in the ministry today. God is so good.

Tom and Lucy Evans were from New Jersey. They had come from very different backgrounds. Tom was raised in a dysfunctional family at an inner city in East Orange. As a child, his parents had no concern for church attendance or God. A lady from his neighborhood would occasionally round up some of the kids in the projects he lived in and take them to church. But things weren't good at home. He first started stealing his father's alcohol at age nine, then began doing drugs at age twelve to escape the horrors of his abusive alcoholic father and verbally abusive mother.

The neighborhood was a ghetto of mainly black African-Americans. As a troubled white boy, Tom experienced severe reverse prejudice as he attended school. He was constantly in conflicts defending himself because of his skin color. It was during the years of great prejudice, just after the assassination of the Rev. Martin Luther King Jr., Tom grew up a half mile from where the infamous Newark riots broke out following the assassination. His life was in relentless danger, and his regard for God was non-existent.

Tom quickly became a product of his environment. Drug use became a way of life for him, where he began to sell drugs at the age of fifteen to support his own habit. He quit school and by seventeen, he was kicked out of his home. At eighteen, he was arrested for the possession of five pounds of marijuana. Due to his age and because it was his first offense, he was given three years' probation for this offense. However, his criminal activity increased over the next few years and he found himself managing a pot warehouse for the Mob. He also got involved with Satanism and developed a deeper interest in the occult world and the power it had on society.

In 1976, at age twenty-one, Tom met Lucy, who was seventeen. Lucy had come from suburbia. Her parents were immigrants from Italy. She lived in a nice neighborhood and went to a good school in Livingston, New Jersey. Lucy was not raised in dysfunction as Tom was. She was raised Catholic but she felt this emptiness inside of her which led her to experiment with drugs which was what other young people were trying in those days. During the sixties and seventies, sex, drugs and rock 'n' roll was rampant. She would occasionally party with her peers.

By her early teens, her involvement with drugs began to grow, along with the pursuit of spiritual fulfillment. She dabbled in occultism and Eastern religions. She had a "hippie/biker" lifestyle. After high school, Lucy's plans for college vanished, much to her parents' anguish, and she moved into Tom's apartment with him.

Not only was Tom managing the "pot warehouse", he was also selling cocaine and so they had plenty of money and all they lived for was fun. In 1979, all this came crashing down as they were arrested. In order to get Lucy off, Tom pleaded guilty and was facing ten to fifteen years imprisonment. About a month after the bust, Lucy found out that she was pregnant. They decided to marry. At this time, Lucy got sober and clean. She started to question the lifestyle they had been living and she wanted to change for her baby. Lucy went for counseling at her church and they told her about the Teen Challenge program. In 1981, both Tom and Lucy asked Christ to forgive them of their sins and they made a commitment to serve him and turn their backs on drugs and the lifestyle of crime.

Louis went to Tom's trial in New Jersey and spoke to the judge on Tom's behalf. Miraculously, the judge sentenced Tom to attend the Bible school and five years' probation. Tom graduated in 1984 and today, Tom and Lucy both have degrees and are pastors of the counseling services at their church. Isn't God an awesome God?

Lester Ortiz was the middle child of three, born into a dysfunctional family. His father was an abusive alcoholic. However, when Lester was still very young, his dad started working part-time for a Catholic church and he became a Christian.

The children could all attend the Catholic school because of their father's job. Although Lester had dyslexia, at the Catholic school, the nuns gave him personal attention to help him with this problem and he did well.

In middle school, he transferred to the public school system and it was here he started to get into trouble. He no longer got individual help with the dyslexia and kids made fun of him, so he got into a lot of fights.

In high school, Lester continued to get into fights and he got caught with marijuana, so he asked his father to allow him to leave school since he was getting into so much trouble. His dad said he could but he had to get a job and work. His father got him a job in the garment factory where both his dad and mother worked, but Lester found more drugs here than when he was in school. He got mixed up with stealing drugs from a drug lord and when they couldn't get the money from Lester, they kidnapped his mom as a ransom. His father had to take a loan from the Catholic church to pay this debt to get his wife back. After this deal was over, Lester was kicked out of his home and told not to come back until he was off drugs.

He lived on the streets for three years. One night, it was freezing cold and he asked a friend to let him sleep in the basement. The friend refused. He asked him if he could have the dog's blanket as he was so cold. Again the friend refused to help him. He realized then that he had no friends.

Lester had gone from being a huge man with a fifty-two-inch waist to a bag of bones with a thirty-two-inch waist. He was sick of his life and truly wanted to change. He had a dream where he was in a cemetery and graves were opening and people were going up to heaven and he was left behind. It really scared him and when he woke up, he went home to his father and said he needed help and wanted to change.

His brother had gone to a Youth Challenge program in New Jersey. Lester called the director there, who accepted him into the induction center. He then came up to the program in Sunbury, Pennsylvania which he completed.

He met Ruth Donato there and two years later, she became his wife.

Ruthie is such a sweetheart. She was born and raised in Brooklyn, New York, and is one of six children. She has a twin brother. She was born into a very abusive home. Her father was the youngest of seventeen children and was an alcoholic and a womanizer. Her mom was a battered woman, but her grandmother was a Christian, who always took her mom and the children to church.

When Ruthie was six years old, she took some change from her mother's purse and went to cross the road to go and buy some candy, without her mother's permission, and was hit by a car. She was hospitalized for two months and not expected to live. Her arm had been so badly broken that the doctor had told her mom she would definitely lose the arm. But God had other plans for Ruth. She not only survived the accident, but she regained full use of her arm as well.

In 1975, Ruth accepted Christ into her life. She found out that her Heavenly Father was not at all like her earthly father, who had given her verbal and physical abuse all her life. It was so good to find out that she was loved.

She had dropped out of school in the tenth grade and gone to work in her father's store and longed to get out of that situation. Her older brother Abe had gone to Bible school and done an internship at Rochester Teen Challenge. He had told Ruth about Teen Challenge Bible Institute. Ruth had such a desire to come to school and learn how to help others from dysfunctional lifestyles; and so, at the age of twenty-three, she applied to Teen Challenge Bible Student as a student and was accepted.

She came by bus from New York City to rural Pennsylvania and was extremely nervous at how she would be accepted. She was concerned because she was Hispanic and also, she was heavy and had always been ridiculed and put down by her father and been told she was unacceptable. She had very little self-esteem. She was met at the bus stop by Florence Ivery, whose first words to her were, "You are the prettiest girl I have ever seen!"

While as a student at Teen Challenge Bible Institute, she learned a lot about love, and understanding and acceptance from a loving God. She received an emotional healing and after her graduation, she stayed on to become part of the staff.

Ruth has a great voice and became the choir director. In 1987, she met Lester who was a student at the men's home. He was attracted to her because of her sweet spirit and Christian values and walk with the Lord. Lester had a nice singing voice himself. He would sing in the choir and he would complement Ruth on her singing and they became friends. They fell in love and in 1989 they were married. This was a dream come true that years before Ruth never believed would become a reality. Today they are both still serving the Lord and helping others.

Norma Sutherland was one of fourteen children born to her mother. Two of her siblings had died at birth. She was the third eldest child and she says her family was very dysfunctional. The family lived with her paternal grandparents at first. Her grandfather molested her from age seven onwards and her father followed in his footsteps.

She said that all the men in her family were abusive, alcoholics and womanizers and treated the women with disrespect and abuse. She remembers her father watching the girls through peep holes while they were getting undressed. He would always tell them how unacceptable they were and ugly and that no man would want them. Not the kind of things a little girl growing up wants to hear from her daddy!

At age eleven, she started running away from home and stealing items out of the stores to survive. When she was thirteen, she was sent to a juvenile detention home where she lived until she was fifteen. Upon her release, she was raped by a twenty-two-year-old man. He pleaded guilty to the crime but because of her background, he got off with just a slap on the wrist.

By age sixteen, Norma started smoking marijuana and doing drugs and at eighteen she was convicted of a murder. She was not guilty of the murder and had been framed. However, because of her rebellious, drug-addicted background and history, she was an easy target and she was sent to Muncy State Prison. Norma spent three years of her sentence there and then she was granted a new trial. At this second trial, she was found not guilty and freed.

At twenty-two, she was addicted to heroin and cocaine. She already had one daughter and her second child was stillborn. A concerned policeman told her about New Life for Girls which is a residential program, like Teen Challenge, to help troubled women. At the time, she was not interested in going there because of the strict rules. But after she had been arrested for prostitution, she was given the choice of going back to prison or to New Life for Girls. She opted to go into this program.

New Life for Girls also had a children's home that could minister to her daughter, while Norma was getting the help she needed. It was here that Norma's life was changed. The people she met were genuine Christians and lived what they were talking about. They were not fakes and genuinely loved her and introduced her to a loving God who thought she was special.

One day she was looking out of the window and she said to God, "I'm tired of living the life I am living, there has to be something better than this. I want to change, so will you please help me?" God heard her prayer and she turned her back on her old life and accepted Christ into her heart that day... life has never been the same since then.

In 1978, Bob and Joyce Sellers were on the verge of divorce when they came to Teen Challenge Bible Institute looking for help. They had three sons and their middle son Rick had been running away from home and getting into trouble from the age of eleven. At age thirteen, Rick continued to be arrested on drug and alcohol-related charges and was in and out of juvenile institutions from 1972 onwards. The courts sent the family to psychiatrists, hospitals, mental health clinics—but with little or no positive effect.

On the advice of one of the psychiatrists, the Sellers moved from Sunbury to Lewisburg, Pennsylvania. Bob even changed his work schedule to day shift to try to make things better in his home, but to no avail.

When they came for counseling at Teen Challenge Bible Institute, Bob and Joyce found a lot of support, encouragement and love there. These new Christian friends began to pray for their family. Louis Correa began visiting Rick in prison. After being released in 1980, Rick told Louis that although he was freed from prison, he still felt like he was locked up inside. Rick received Christ into his life that night and asked him for forgiveness and told God that if he could do anything with a messed up life like his, he was ready to surrender it to God. That was a Thursday night and by Saturday, Louis had him on a plane headed to a program in Georgia. After graduating from that rehabilitation program, he went on to the second phase at Rehrersburg, Pennsylvania and then on to the Bible school.

He graduated from Bible school and today has a good job and is still serving God, who changed his life completely. Rick will tell you this...that everyone is unique but they all have one thing in common: a God-hole in their hearts! There is only one answer to this problem and that is God. We all have a sinful nature and only God can change a man. He is grateful that God changed his heart and gave him a new life.

God is still in the business of changing lives today. Maybe you need a miracle in your life and need a change. God is waiting to welcome you into his family and give you a life worth living. If you need this miracle, today is the day to make that decision. Life is so short, don't waste it. Give your life to God and you will see how much better you will feel. Your problems may not all disappear but you will have the joy of the Lord to be your strength; God will help you through this life so you will never have to be alone again. The wonderful miracles of changed lives we heard as the new students came into the school each semester were inspiring. We saw how God continued to change these damaged lives and how he made something beautiful and useful out of them. It made our ministry at the Bible school fulfilling and gratifying, knowing that we were able to be an influence and an encouragement to these students. In the three years they stayed at the Bible school, we saw them develop into men and women of God with a mission in their hearts—to reach out and help others who were hurting just like they had been, before meeting the Lord and having their whole lives gloriously changed.

RAISING OUR FAMILY AT TEEN CHALLENGE

CATHERINE RETURNS TO THE UNITED STATES:

My mother returned from Africa after spending several years there with Heather and her family. Teen Challenge Institute employed her as a librarian and an instructor. She lived in a small trailer on campus so she had her independence. She loved her position and was an inspiration to the students and staff alike. Raelene Kenzy told us that she felt called to do missionary work from hearing the many true stories my mom would tell of her life in Africa and the missionary work there.

We were happy to have my Mom so close. She would always introduce Louis as her son-in-love instead of son-in-law and we were truly blessed to have her in our lives. She had lots of energy and was willing to help wherever there was a need. Louis loved her as if she were his own mother and included her in all our outings and vacations. She went through major heart bypass surgery in the years she lived at the school, but bounced back, continuing to live and work there.

In 1986, Catherine met and married Harry Shumaker. Harry was the owner of Quality Print Shop in Sunbury and had been a widower for two and a half years. His wife and oldest daughter had been killed in a tragic accident and he was lonely. He met Catherine when she went to pay a bill for the school and they soon became friends. Harry's younger daughter and family welcomed Catherine into the family. They were happy that Harry would have companionship and not be lonely anymore.

Catherine continued to work at the school for the first year of her marriage and she also taught Sunday school at Harry's church. After some time, she gave up her position at the school since she had more cardiac surgery. She had another heart attack and needed stents placed. She was also told she only had a third of her heart functioning. Catherine was a fighter and she came through the operation well and, after she recuperated, she continued to work faithfully for the Lord.

CATHERINE CONTINUES TO BEAT DEATH:

Catherine then had a stroke. At the hospital, they were doing a blind study on people who had strokes. She took the medicine which worked for her and she was left without any serious defects, for which we praised the Lord.

However, she was living on a third of her heart and having to take large doses of medicine to keep her alive. She got medication, later acquired Parkinson's disease, and began to fall. One doctor had told her she would not be alive for her next appointment, but she fooled them all and lived for five years more after that statement.

OUR CHILDREN:

In November 1976, God blessed us again with another precious son, Jonmark Stephen Correa. Jason was already six years old and Nigel three and a half, so they were out of the baby stage. I so enjoyed having another little baby. Like my first two sons, Jonmark was a gift from God whom I treasured. I immensely enjoyed my sons' childhood years.

My children, along with the other staff children on campus, had happy childhoods playing together. The grounds on which the school was located allowed them ample places to ride their bikes and build forts and there was a playground for them to play in. In the winter time, there were places for them to sled and build snowmen and have snowball fights. They were joyful children and always had playmates. They would play different games like kick the can and Army, and they would also build forts. As they grew, they enjoyed playing baseball, learning how to bowl and swim and play basketball. They also enjoyed normal sports activities at the public schools they attended.

Each night we would have family devotions with them and they loved for me to read Bible stories to them. They would say their prayers before going to sleep. I remember during one of these times of family devotions that Jason had just gotten over the chicken pox and now

Nigel had them. Nigel sincerely prayed to God to give them back to Jason as he didn't want them! So, you can see these times were times we could teach our children godly principles as we told him that you were not to ask God to bring any kind of evil on anyone.

One time Jason and Nigel ran off to play with their friends and left Jonmark alone and he was very sad that they didn't want him to go along. Louis explained to him that is what happens sometimes when you are younger. Louis then invited Jonmark to go and play table tennis with him. Jonmark was delighted to get some alone time with his Dad. All my boys are wonderful with children. I believe it is because they learned that from their father. He always tried to take time to talk to and encourage his children even though the ministry took most of his time away from them.

I believe that no matter what my children have to go through in this life, the spiritual foundation they were given as children goes with them. The prayers and faith of their parents and grandmother will follow them all the days of their lives and will keep them and give them strength to endure anything they have to face.

I remember when Louis would pray for people at the altar; Jason would stand by his side and pray right along with his Dad. One day, when he was about five years old, he had his eyes tightly shut and put his little hand on a lady that had come to the front for prayer and I heard him say, "Please heal this woman, Lord!" He was following in his father's footsteps but I believe God heard his prayers because he was sincere and he loved God.

One day our friend Bob had hurt his finger and asked Nigel to pray for him. The next day his finger was all healed so he went to show Nigel his finger. Nigel was not surprised by what he saw and asked Bob what had he expected from God? That is why the Bible tells us to have the faith of a little child. So many times we pray for things but do not really pray with expectations. God tells us in the Bible that we are to become like little children who come to God with believing hearts. Children believe what you tell them and so are full of faith and expect God to do whatever they ask him to do.

"Whosoever therefore shall humble himself as this little child, the same is greatest in the kingdom of heaven" Matthew 18:4 (KJV)

God Keeps His Hand on Jonmark:

When Jonmark was three years old, I was given a trip to go and visit my twin sister in South Africa. Louis stayed at home with the two oldest boys and I took Jonmark with me. It was Christmas Eve and we were getting ready for the service at our church in South Africa when my brother-in-law came into the house soaking wet. Behind him stood Jonmark also soaking wet!

We found out that Jonmark had sneaked out of the house to go and sail his little boat in the swimming pool and had fallen into the deep end of the pool. Although he had taken swimming lessons at the YMCA and knew how to swim somewhat, he did not have the common sense to turn around and swim to the shallow end to get out. He had wearied himself out and was about to drown. My brother in-law was walking out to go to the car when he heard Jonmark's cries and quickly dove into the water and saved his life. I am so glad God takes care of us. What a tragedy that would have been to find our baby dead in the pool.

I thanked God for the scripture in Isaiah 43:2:

"When thou passest through the waters, I will be with thee; and through the rivers, they shall not overflow thee: when thou walkest through the fire, thou shalt not be burned: neither shall the flame kindle upon thee." Isaiah 43:2 (KJV)

My children loved having their granny close by and every Friday night would ask to sleep over in her trailer. She would get up and make them a special breakfast on Saturday mornings of scrambled eggs and toast and orange juice. She was a great storyteller and so they would ask her to tell them stories which kept them entertained. She also spoiled them when they missed the school bus. Instead of coming home to me to tell me they had missed the school bus, they would run over to their granny who would quickly get dressed and take them to school so they would not get into trouble.

Every year, the school had a walkathon and our children faithfully collected names of people to sponsor them. When others gave up on the long walk, the boys persevered and always finished that walk. I was so proud of each one of them for their perseverance and effort they put forth. They learned the principle of not giving up when times get hard.

NOTHING IS TOO BIG OR
SMALL FOR GOD TO DO:

The boys had bikes and mini motorbikes. Lester, who was a mechanic, would help them fix them up and maintain them. One day they tried to show their dad how to ride their motorbike. The boys explained to their father how to ride a motorbike, but Louis did not know that he should use the one hand as the clutch and the other hand as the accelerator. They said he took off and did a "popper wheelie," which made him go straight up in the air. He then came back down and fell off the cycle and it landed on top of him. I gave them strict instructions they were to remember their dad was a city boy and older now, so they should not let him near their motorbike. They all had a good laugh after they knew their dad was not seriously hurt.

HOME MISSIONS:

We were living in the United States but we were home missionaries. We did not have much money and had difficulties and trials to go through like all people do. Although not enjoyable at the time, I believe what we went through taught our boys life lessons that made them the men they are today. Trials come to all of us and we have to learn to adjust and go on in life.

Every year the school would have problems with the sewer and water system for at least one week out of the year, usually it would be in the summer time. We would have to go to the YMCA or over the road to the Kenzy's home to take showers as we did not have water. The toilets would not flush either. We would have to get buckets of water from a water truck that the city loaned to us to flush them manually until the problem was solved.

It seemed like a yearly thing also that the heating system would fail. The building would get so cold. We laughed about it later but I remember one of our staff members telling me how it was so cold in her apartment that one day she got dressed to go downtown complete with winter boots and coat. When she got to town, the sun was out and everyone else was dressed in shorts and summer clothes and she was dressed up for winter weather!

I guess the pilgrims of old experienced the same trials that we were having. The Bible tells us not to complain about our circumstances. Although most of us did grumble at the time, I believe we learned to be more compassionate for those in third world countries that put up with these things or worse on a daily basis. We needed to be thankful that we just had to experience these problems occasionally, rather than daily.

THANK YOU GOD FOR THE FOOD WE EAT:

Most of our meals were served in the cafeteria and we ate whatever the Lord sent in for us to eat. Many times we would get calls to say trucks had broken down and people wanted to know if we could use bread or some other items or someone's freezer had been broken and could we use some frozen items. We were also given deer meat and one time we were given live turkeys that we had to kill, pluck, and prepare for the freezer. Some farmers came to help us prepare the turkeys. After the staff and students were involved in that effort, we didn't want to eat turkey for a while!

Many churches would donate food and other organizations would send us delicious leftovers from banquets they had held. We also received donations to purchase food items, so we never went hungry. Although I cooked some meals at home, especially on the weekends, my children had to learn to eat what was served in the cafeteria during the week. All these trials taught my sons to be the men they are today.

PRISON MINISTRIES:

Although we did not have much money since the school depended on donations to operate, we enjoyed the ministry. God opened the door for Louis to go into the prisons both locally and then into the federal penitentiaries in Lewisburg and Allenwood, to hold services for the Spanish-speaking population. He was able to use his fluency in Spanish and his past life experiences to relate to these men. Louis had been where they were and understood what they were going through. Many men gave their lives to the Lord through Louis's faithful ministry from 1975 until he went to be with the Lord.

A MIRACLE OF FINANCES:

Because we did not get paid on a regular basis and we were raising a family, we had acquired some debt. In 1989, I left my position as the business manager for the Teen

Challenge Institute and took a job in a nursing home as an aide.

We also decided after prayer that I would go back to school to become a nurse. We had no money for me to go to school. We prayed and I applied to Geisinger School of Nursing as a student. I was in my forties and was nervous about becoming a student again. I asked God for his favor and his help as I knew in myself I was taking on something big. My children were all teenagers, and, along with my husband, they encouraged me to take this step.

I found out about the scholarship program and I applied for it. I asked God for a miracle. He answered our prayers and gave me that miracle! I was given a scholarship that paid for my schooling in exchange for my working weekends as an aide for a year and then working for them for a period of time after graduation. What an answer to prayer that was.

In order to qualify as a student, I had to take the entrance exams. I needed remedial chemistry and algebra to pass this test. I took a short refresher course in algebra and chemistry at the local high school. I was blessed by a friend, John Traver, who was a high school chemistry teacher and tutored me in simple chemistry. I passed the test with God's help. I took some courses in the summer at Bloomsburg University and a few correspondence courses through Pennsylvania State University. As a result, when I entered Geisinger School of Nursing, my course work was mostly nursing courses. That made my load lighter since I was working the 3–11 shift Fridays through Sundays and still had to take care of a home and family.

I didn't know anyone attending nursing school and, as a non-traditional student, I asked God to give me a friend and someone to study with. He did just that for me. Megan King was also a non-traditional student attending school. It was in the first semester shortly after we started nursing school that Megan went to see her mother and found her on the bathroom floor having suffered an aneurysm. The death of her mother was devastating. It was through this tragedy that Megan and I became best friends as I sought to comfort her. Megan says her faith in God grew during this time.

We spent a lot of time studying, laughing and sometimes crying together as we encouraged one another through those difficult years of studying, working and balancing family life. God was faithful to us. In 1993, we graduated as registered nurses and started working at Geisinger Hospital in Danville, Pennsylvania.

My twin came over from Africa for my graduation and we even got a small write up in the local newspaper. My brother and sister-in-law came from Canada and I had a big party to celebrate. It was also our twenty-fifth wedding anniversary so we had a lot to celebrate that year.

Little did I know back then but God was preparing me to have a good job to support myself when Louis would pass away in 1998.

RULES, RELIGION AND RELATIONSHIP:

Although we were very busy at the school, we still managed to get away every year to take a vacation, even if it were only a few miles from home. Our children enjoyed their growing up years, but when they became teenagers, we ran into some problems.

As our children got older, they faced problems that other children not living on campus did not have to confront. While they enjoyed youth group camp on campus, they were constantly being preached to by our students. They heard a lot about hell and damnation and so felt a great deal of fear concerning their futures.

Whereas I grew up very naïve concerning different lifestyles and drug addiction, my children grew up surrounded by people who were from dysfunctional families or were from the drug and alcohol and gang lifestyles and backgrounds. Hearing the students' stories all the time, I think, numbed them to the awfulness of such lifestyles. It became familiar to my children and, at times, the stories they heard made taking drugs, partying, etc., something exciting to do.

The rules for the Teen Challenge students were strict because of their previous lifestyles. They were learning how to conduct themselves as ministers of the Gospel. The students had many restrictions while they were going to school. They were not allowed to go to town to watch movies or go to dances. The men could not grow their hair long or go to other social functions that were not associated with Teen Challenge. They also had chapel every day and a mandatory service every Friday evening.

Because we lived on campus and were part of the staff, our children came under these strict rules even though they were not students there. As our children got older, they rebelled against such rules since all of their school friends were going places and doing things they were prohibited from going. Every Friday evening, they were expected to attend the service at Teen Challenge with the family. The preaching was geared to students going into ministry. The service emphasized doctrine and study material which our children felt was long and boring and covered topics to which they could not relate. They wanted to spend their time with their school friends doing normal school activities.

Hindsight is always better than foresight. Years later, I had to apologize to my children for keeping them from experiencing some of their normal school functions. Although we were very sincere in what we believed in and thought we were doing right, we did not realize we were teaching them more about rules and regulations and the judgments of God instead of God's amazing love.

Without us knowing it, there was also a more serious problem that our children faced. While most of the students were sincerely trying to change their ways, there were a few who were sneaking out to engage in their old lifestyles of drinking and doing drugs. My children were aware of this double standard. They saw these same students giving testimonies of how God had changed them and they knew of their backsliding and so they saw hypocrisy in the school and church.

Another problem that they faced was some of the teenage children of the married Teen Challenge students and alumni would visit the campus. Some of them were experimenting with drugs and introduced these to the teens on campus. We thought we were raising our children in a protective environment but the devil knows how to influence each one of us and he will find a way to try to destroy our families if he can.

In case you think these things only happen in places like Teen Challenge, you are highly mistaken. When interviewing my adult children for this book, they told me that there were others who were from good homes that attended school with them who were also inquisitive to find out about drugs. They too would experiment with marijuana and the drug scene. Their parents, like us, did not have a clue of what was going on.

I believe we need to pray daily for our families. I dedicated my children to God when they were first born and gave them back to the Lord. I remind him daily that he cannot lose what I gave to him for safekeeping.

"And they said, Believe on the Lord Jesus Christ, and thou shalt be saved, and thy house." Acts 16:31 (KJV)

The world today is a more dangerous world to live in for children than when we were raising our children. The Internet has opened up even more traps for our kids to get involved with. We need to teach our children what is right and wrong but, above all, we need to share with them how much Jesus loves them. They need to know that religion is boring and restricting, but a relationship with Jesus is exciting and freeing.

The Bible tells us in Proverbs 22:6:

"Train up a child in the way he should go: and when he is old, he will not depart from it." Proverbs 22:6 (KJV)

Today's parents are more aware of predators and pitfalls than we were aware of them and are not as naïve as parents of my generation were. It is imperative that we pray for our children and grandchildren and that they learn they have a friend in Jesus who will be with them wherever they go. They need to know that being a Christian is a wonderful, enjoyable way of life and not one that is just rules and regulations. We as parents need to trust God with our children and know that God is in control and will take care of them. When we do our part, we can be sure that God will do his part and our household shall be saved.

BALANCE:

The Bible teaches balance. Looking back on what my children faced growing up, there was a lack of balance in some areas. They received too much religion and rules and saw hypocrisy in those that were weak. Because of the strict rules that we followed, they also felt there was too much control.

When they were old enough, they swung over to the other side and tried the alcohol and drugs for themselves. Then, when they left home, they did not attend church because they felt organized religion was not for real. So they went from one side of the pendulum of life to the opposite side, but it is God's desire for us to stay in the middle and live a balanced life.

Many young people are leaving the church for the same reasons. The devil tries to trick them into believing we have to be religious to go to heaven but this is a lie. Following strict rules and trying to be perfect, never allowing yourself to have fun and growing up thinking if you do anything against those rules will send you to hell forever, instills fear of judgment into you. Since this is no way to live, young people are just giving up on the church. But, they are still seeking fulfillment in life and they try to find it in the world. God made us all with a desire for Him and nothing in this world will satisfy us until we come to peace with God and surrender our lives to Him.

The Bible says Jesus came to give us abundant life and that he wants us to enjoy life not to live in fear. Although there are absolutes in the Bible that all men must adhere to, being a Christian is not following rules and regulations but it is having a wonderful relationship with an awesome God. When you have this type of relationship, God will let you know when he does not want you to be involved in certain activities. As you read the Bible, you will find answers to your questions. He will put it on your conscience if you are doing something wrong. You will feel uneasy participating because you do not want to displease the Lord in any way.

When you read the Old Testament, men had to follow strict rules and offer up sacrifices to God to have their sins forgiven. It was called living under the dispensation of the law. Thank God we do not live under that dispensation anymore. God sent Jesus to be our Savior and now we live under the dispensation of grace. We no longer have to try to be good enough and worry that we are not going to make it because we are not perfect.

Jesus criticized the Pharisees because they were religious and did not have the proper relationship with God. He told them that it is not rules, regulations and religion that please God. It is a personal relationship with a personal God.

Jesus said he came to this world to give us life more abundantly and to take away the fear and sting of death. Hell was never made for man but for Satan and his demons. The only way man goes to hell is if he refuses to accept the gift of eternal life from Jesus. Jesus came to pay the price for our sins and to forgive us so that we would never have to join Satan and his demons in hell. He gave his life on the cross for anyone who will accept him into their lives and accept his forgiveness and the gift of eternal life from him which he offers freely to all who will come to him.

The Bible teaches us that the little children came running to Jesus and the parents brought their children to him to be blessed. That tells me that he was not a person who was rigid or strict but one who was loving, gentle and kind, and that people enjoyed being around him.

The Bible says that everywhere he went, he did good and that he loved to heal the sick and set the captives free. This is the God that the Bible wants us to get to know. He is not waiting to punish us or bring judgment down on us. He is waiting with open arms ready to bless us and give us a good life down here and eternity with him in heaven forever when we die. All he wants is our love and fellowship and for us to put him first in our lives. Then, we are to love others and share the good news of the Gospel with them. The reason God created us is so we could have fellowship with him.

"The thief cometh not, but for to steal, and to kill, and to destroy: I am come that they might have life, and that they might have it more abundantly." John 10:10 (KJV)

God does not want us to struggle everyday and be unhappy. He made us to be spiritual, physical, and social beings. He wants us to find balance and fulfillment in each of these areas. It is when we lose balance in these areas that we lose our purpose in life and Satan can make us feel frustrated, depressed and sad. Satan will attack us in each of these areas so that we will not accomplish God's plan for our lives. But we can become aware of his tactics and determine to get back into balance and live our lives with purpose for our Lord.

"For I know the thoughts that I think toward you, saith the Lord, thought of peace, and not of evil, to give you an expected end." Jeremiah 29:11 (KJV)

From this verse, we see that God definitely has a purpose for us while we live down here on earth. Do not allow Satan to lie to you and tell you anything different.

SATAN IS A LIAR:

Satan has fooled mankind into thinking God is a vengeful, judgmental God who is out to get us when we make mistakes. Satan is a liar. We have the privilege to serve an awesome God who is filled with mercy and grace. He does not want us to feel condemned or forsaken. When we make mistakes and we acknowledge them to him and ask for his forgiveness, he does so immediately. He casts our sins into the sea of forgetfulness and does not hold them against us anymore. God says we are precious to him and that he has a good plan for our lives. The Bible says that he goes to and fro on earth looking for those who he can bless. Yes, his purpose is to bless us, to give us favor and not to condemn us.

Although my children felt they lived with too much religion, I believe they saw true relationship with God in their parents and grandmother and others they knew who sincerely and wholeheartedly loved God. They have all told me that they appreciate their home life and the principles of life they were taught growing up.

My children are adults today with their own families. They are hard workers, faithful husbands, and good upright citizens. God has indeed poured out his blessings on them. I am very proud of the wonderful men they have grown up to be.

MAJOR CHANGES

In 1995, after graduation, Jonmark decided to go into the Army. We were very proud of him wanting to serve his country. Because of his duty to his country, he had to miss his brother's wedding which I know was a big disappointment for him.

In 1995, Jason married his college sweetheart Renee. Renee is a wonderful wife to him and a great daughter-in-law. She had been raised in the Catholic faith with many rules to follow and so was not attending church by the time she was in college. Like many young people, she was searching for something real and being religious was not hitting the mark. Although she was not practicing her religion, she says she believed in God and loved him. She had never experienced drugs and was shocked to see many of the college kids experimenting with drugs when she went to college. Thank God she never had a desire to try them for herself.

Shortly after Jason and Renee's wedding, Louis had a heart attack and needed open heart bypass surgery. The Lord brought him through that. About a year after his recuperation, Louis decided that he would continue as the contract Spanish chaplain at the prisons but he would give up his position at the school. We had been at Teen Challenge for twenty-two years and seen God work many miracles in that time. Ruined lives had been changed and many of our prayers had been answered.

OUR FIRST HOME:

In 1997, Louis was sixty-two years old and could now take his social security. With that money and with the check he received from the prison and with my job, we had enough money coming in monthly to put a down payment on a small home in Danville, Pennsylvania. It was our first home and we were thrilled to be able to live there. It had an above ground pool in the back garden and flower beds around the house and we fell in love with it. Louis enjoyed watering the garden and we felt so blessed to live there. It was just five minutes from where I worked and not too far from the prisons where Louis worked. Little did we know that Louis had only a year to enjoy his home before the Lord would call him home to his eternal reward and to a much better place.

SUDDEN DEATH:

Louis had not been feeling very well and was experiencing some abdominal discomfort. He visited his doctor; x-rays were taken and other tests done to try to find out what the problem was. All the tests were coming back negative so the doctor had made an appointment for him to see a specialist. However, before we could make that appointment, on August 15, 1998, we went out for supper but Louis could not eat very much because of abdominal pain. When we got home, he went into the bathroom and he passed out on the floor. I called 911 and the ambulance came and took him to the emergency room at Geisinger. They had revived him and started an IV but he was in a lot of pain. The doctor told me they would have to take him to the operating room as he was bleeding internally. I quickly kissed him good-bye and told him I would see him as soon as the operation was done. They rushed him to do emergency surgery.

I called my parents who joined me in the waiting room. A couple hours later, the surgeon came into the room to give us an update. His words were, "I'm sorry, but when we opened up your husband, we found his liver was full of cancer. It had grown out and attacked the aorta. There was nothing we could do to stop the bleeding." I asked him how long Louis had to live and he said, "About an hour." Louis had shown no signs of having liver problems. His skin or the whites of his eyes had not turned yellow so we had no warning that he had liver problems or that he had cancer.

I was numb with shock. Nigel was moving down to North Carolina and Jonmark was helping him move. There was no way to contact them until they reached their destination. I called Jason, who was living about an hour away in Harrisburg. It was in the middle of August and he had his air conditioner on high and did not hear the phone. I knew his wife Renee was visiting her Mom in the Poconos but could not remember her maiden name to contact her. Eventually, I did get hold of Renee who called the police to knock on Jason's door and let him know the news. They were able to keep Louis alive, though heavily sedated and on life support, until Jason and Renee got to my side. Along with my parents and a few close friends, we said our good-byes to my beloved husband.

On August 3, 1998, Louis and I had celebrated our thirtieth wedding anniversary. I had fallen in love with him when I was eighteen and we had had a happy marriage.

It was hard to say good-bye to my best friend and husband. I am glad I had my parents, friends and children around to give me support and love.

Nigel and Jonmark found out the following day about the death of their dad and they turned around and came straight back home to be with the family.

THE FUNERAL:

I was so glad that the Lord had allowed Louis to live until our sons had become men. At the private family viewing, at the funeral home the night before the funeral, they were able to reminisce about the good times growing up with their dad. Knowing they have a lot of happy memories about their father warms my heart.

Jason and Renee helped me make the arrangements and choose a casket. Pastor Helman and my church family and friends all rallied around us, bringing food and cards to the home and giving their condolences. My brother and sister-in-law arrived from Canada and my parents were supportive. Teen Challenge had been given some cemetery plots and John Kenzy gave one of these sites to us for Louis to be laid to rest.

We were amazed to see how many people turned up for the funeral. People not only came from local areas, but arrived from Connecticut, New Jersey, and Florida. The church was packed. Chaplains, who came from the different prisons, brought with them notes and cards from the prisoners, all saying how much they loved and appreciated Louis and how much they were going to miss him. They stated that they knew that no matter what the weather was, Louis would faithfully show up for all scheduled meetings at the prison. There were so many people there that the police came and gave us an escort to the cemetery. My sons were very impressed with this.

Throughout the years, Louis had been faithful to his calling. His sons all commented to me that what impressed them about their dad the most was that so many people respected him because he was genuine and honest and not fake. At his funeral, we all wrote tributes in honor of Louis. These tributes talked about his life of sacrifice, how he lived what he believed in, and how he always had a word of encouragement to pass on. He truly was an example of what it means to be a Christian.

"Thou shalt also decree a thing, and it shall be established unto thee: and the light shall shine upon thy ways." Job 22:28 (KJV)

Louis and I had decreed and declared from their birth that our sons would serve the Lord and become the mighty, powerful men doing exploits for God and walking in his perfect plan that he has destined for them.

Louis went to his grave with this assurance and I know one day we will all be together again in heaven.

LIFE AFTER EXPERIENCING DEATH OF YOUR SPOUSE:

"He healeth the broken in heart, and bindeth up their wounds." Psalm 147:3 (KJV)

I had never lived alone as an adult. Heather and I shared an apartment together before I was married and then I lived with my husband. I was now on my own and, like my mother when she lost my father; I learned to trust in God and get to know him more intimately in the next two years of my life.

After a week, I returned to work at the hospital and had a patient that had diabetes and had lost his sight and part of his leg. Louis had diabetes and I thought how terrible it would have been if he would have found himself in this condition and not have been able to get out to minister and read and study the Word like he enjoyed doing. I then saw a patient who had liver cancer and how he was in so much pain that he had to be kept on a morphine pump to make the pain more bearable. I thought to myself that Louis would have hated to have finished his life back on drugs after God had delivered him over thirty-four years ago.

I remembered the story Pastor Flewellyn had told my mother when my father had died. It helped me to realize that God is sovereign and has a perfect plan for each of our lives; and, when we have fulfilled that plan, he takes us to be with him to a better place.

DELIVERANCE FROM FEAR:

Looking back on my life, I had not realized how fearful I was until after Louis died. When I was growing up in Africa and the Africans would riot, they would paint their faces and play their drums. I was so afraid they would attack our house and we would all be killed. If my mother was late coming home from work, I would have all the lights in the house on and the radios and TV blaring until she got home. Whenever I would visit Heather in Africa, I would make sure I was inside a room, so if there was a break-in, I would be safe.

In our church they had a prayer team that would pray for those who came up to the altar at the end of the service who wanted prayer. In order to be on the team, you had to watch a set of tapes on how to serve in this position. As I was watching these tapes, the minister was explaining how some people are very anxious and afraid and that it could be from a spirit of fear attaching itself to your soul area from when you were a child.

"For God hath not given us the spirit of fear, but of power, and of love, and of a sound mind." 2 Timothy 1:7 (KJV)

The minister said you need to pray and tell that spirit to leave you since you are a child of God. God does not give us a spirit of fear. I did not believe Christians could be affected by evil spirits. When I prayed that night, I said to the Lord, "If this is true and this fear I have is from a spirit that attached itself to my soul area when I was a child, then in the morning when I have my devotions I want it to say something about fear." I then went to bed.

The next morning, I picked up my devotional book to read the daily devotion and it was on the Apostle Paul's conversion. It said that God told Ananias to go and pray for Saul. Ananias was *afraid* to go because of the things Saul had been doing to the Christians, but God told him not to be afraid because he had changed Saul and called him to do a great work for him.

I kneeled down by my bedside and said a simple prayer. "I am a child of God and in the name of Jesus, I tell you spirit of fear that you have no right to bother me and I tell you to go and never come back into my soul area again." God answered my prayer instantly of all fear of being alone left and I am not fearful anymore.

DREAMS:

One night shortly after Louis died, I had a dream. I was being chased by a big man and he was trying to catch me and harm me. Suddenly I was surrounded by a group of people. This man could not get to me and he had to leave me alone. Then the dream changed and I saw myself sitting in a wheelchair. I was hurt and unable to defend myself and once again I was being chased by this angry man. But, as he got close to me, I was surrounded by a group of people and this enemy had to leave again because he could not get to me.

I asked the Lord what the dream meant and he showed me how I was like that young girl, who was hurt and felt alone. But he was going to surround me with friends and family who would help me through this difficult time in

my life and that I was going to be all right. The next day
I read Psalm 91 which brought me peace.

> He that dwelleth in the secret place of the
> most High shall abide under the shadow of the
> Almighty.
>
> I will say of the Lord, He is my refuge and
> my fortress :my God; in him will I trust.
>
> Surely he shall deliver thee from the snare
> of the fowler, and from the noisome pestilence.
>
> He shall cover thee with his feathers, and
> under his wings shalt thou trust: his truth shall
> be thy shield and buckler.
>
> Thou shalt not be afraid for the terror by
> night; nor for the arrow that flieth by day;
>
> Nor for the pestilence that walketh in
> darkness; not for the destruction that wasteth
> at noonday.
>
> A thousand shall fall at your side, and ten
> thousand at thy right hand; but it shall not
> come by thee.
>
> Only with thine eyes shalt thou behold and
> see the reward of the wicked.
>
> Because thou hast made the Lord, which is
> my refuge, even the most High, thy habitation;
>
> There shall no evil befall thee, neither shall
> any plague come nigh thy dwelling.
>
> For he shall give his angels charge over
> thee, to keep thee in all thy ways.
>
> They shall bear thee up in their hands, lest
> thou dash thy foot against a stone.
>
> Thou shalt tread upon the lion and the
> adder: the young lion and the dragon shalt thou
> trample under feet.

> Because he has set his love upon me,
> therefore will I deliver him: I will set him on
> high, because he hath known my name.
> He shall call upon me, and I will answer
> him: I will deliver him, and honour him.
> With long life will I satisfy him, and shew
> him my salvation."

Psalm 91 (KJV)

GOD GIVES ME A PERSONAL PROPHECY:

Three months after Louis died, I was invited to go with a group of people from our church who was going away for four days to another church that was holding special revival meetings. I decided to go along. I am so glad I did because I had an experience on that trip that was such an encouragement to me.

I was standing in the service singing and praising God when it felt like someone pushed me back and I found myself sitting in my seat. No one had touched me or was speaking to me but I heard a voice saying to me the following: "I know who you are; I know your name. I will take you through this time of mourning and grief but it will not be long and it will not overwhelm you. I will restore ministry to your life and new love and your latter days will be greater than your former days." Today, God has done exactly what that prophecy said he would do for me.

One day sometime after this experience, I was feeling down and missing my husband and I went to visit a lady in a nursing home. As I sat in the car before going into the home, I said to the Lord, "You told me that this grief and mourning would not overwhelm me. I am feeling so overwhelmed at this moment!"

I had my eyes closed as I was uttering this heartfelt prayer to God. The next thing I knew it was twenty minutes later. I opened my eyes and I felt peace and that turmoil was all gone. I felt that at that moment the Lord had called Louis over and told him to give his wife a hug because she desperately needed one at that moment. I was able to dry my tears and go in and encourage someone else because God had encouraged me.

"He shall call upon me, and I will answer him: I will be with him in trouble; I will deliver him, and honour him." Psalm 91:15 (KJV)

THE BATTLE RAGES:

Nigel and his fiancé were married in November 1998. They decided to return from North Carolina and moved in with me. It was nice having the company; however, I soon found out that Nigel had some serious life-controlling problems and was involved with drugs and alcohol.

For the next twelve years, he would struggle with these issues. It was a very trying time for me and I prayed earnestly for God to deliver him from this lifestyle. It put a strain on their marriage and he and his wife ended up getting a divorce. There were court cases and counseling sessions during this time and we kept on believing that one day Nigel would change his life.

In Luke 15, we read a story about a man who asked his father for his inheritance and then he went off into faraway land and wasted everything on riotous living. While he had money, he had many friends; but when all his money was gone, he was alone and had nothing. He had to take a job taking care of pigs and even had to eat the pig food. For a Jewish man, this was the lowest of all jobs.

One day this man, who the Bible calls the prodigal son, took an inventory of his life. He said to himself that he was going to return to his father's house and beg his father to take him back as a hired servant. He did not feel worthy to ask to be taken back as a son.

The father had been praying for his wayward son since he had left home, and the story relates that, when his son was still far away, the father saw him coming and ran out to meet him. His son was making his humble statement to his dad. However, the father was so glad to see him that he told his servants to bring him a clean robe. He put a ring on his son's finger and held a big party to celebrate his son's return. He said, "My son who was dead is alive again."

In (2011), Nigel was serving a six-month sentence for a DUI and like his father, years before, he had a true experience with God. He told me he knew that no one had sent him to jail but God. He was at the bottom of the pit and had nowhere else to go. Like the prodigal son, he had wasted his life. He was in his mid-thirties and had nothing to show for his life because of the drugs and alcohol. He asked God to forgive him and he determined in his heart that day to return to the faith of his father and serve God.

While he was in jail, Nigel gave his testimony to many of the other inmates who also repented and accepted Jesus into their lives. When he got out of jail, he went back to church and he turned his back on the drugs and alcohol. He is keeping his eyes on the Lord and fulfilling the following scripture:

> "Not as if I had already attained, either were already perfect: but I follow after, if that I may apprehend that for which also I am apprehended of Christ Jesus.
>
> Brethren, I count not myself to have apprehended but this one thing I do, forgetting those things that are behind, and reaching forth unto those things which are before,
>
> I press toward the mark for the prize of the high calling of God in Christ Jesus."
>
> Philippians 3:12-14 (KJV)

Once again we thank God for the second chances he gives us all when we truly repent and ask him to forgive us and we call out to him sincerely for help.

New Beginnings

A group of people in our church rallied around me while I was adjusting to life as a widow and single adult. Just like in the dream I had, God surrounded me with friends to ease the loneliness and to help me adjust to life without Louis. One of these friends was a man named Marvin Snyder who invited me to come out to eat with this group of people and to attend the different functions they had. Being involved with these nice people, who quickly became my friends, helped meet the social needs I had.

Marvin was born to Guy J. and Margaret I. Hoch Snyder, and was the seventh of eight children. His one sister, June, had passed away as a child before Marvin was born. He was raised in a God-fearing, happy home on a farm where he was taught moral and biblical standards and the value of hard work. His parents attended church weekly with their children and it was at their church that he made a decision to accept Christ into his life.

After high school graduation, he served in the Army National Guard. In 1966, he and his younger brother Paul became partners and purchased a farm and worked together for the next twenty-five years.

In 1968, Marvin got married and he and his wife had two children: a daughter in 1969 named Janel and a son in 1971 named Stacy. They raised their family in the same manner they were raised. When the children were old enough, they helped with the farm work. They collected eggs from the fifty-thousand-chicken-layer house. They helped unload hay for their one-hundred-head cow herd and helped with other farm chores. They had a happy, active home. There was always something to do.

Besides farming, from 1972 through 1990, Marvin served on several committees, such as on the Line Mountain School Board, and he also served as a director on both the Northumberland County Farmers Association and the Pennsylvania State Farmers Association. He was also involved as a Sunday school teacher and on the board in the Lutheran church where they attended. Life was busy and life was good.

TWO FREAKY FARMING ACCIDENTS AND GOD'S PROTECTION:

In March 1972, Marvin was spring cleaning the apple orchard and took a broken down tree to the woodland. At the woodlands, he saw a twenty-foot steel shaft lying on the ground that he thought would be good to use for the grapevines to grow on. He put a chain around it and hooked it to the tractor and slowly started driving around the trees.

What he did not realize was that the front end of the shaft stuck into the ground and the tractor acted as a lever. Suddenly, the twenty-foot steel shaft flew up to the tractor's seat. By a miracle Marvin turned around just before the steel bar hit him and raised his left arm to protect himself. The shaft hit his arm and broke it, but it would have killed him if it had hit the back of his head with such force. Although his arm took a long time to recover, he was thankful to God for saving his life.

In 1988, when Stacy was just sixteen years old, God protected him also from a farming accident that could have killed him. It was a very hot and dry season and Stacy was working in the fields. He was pulling a heavy load with the tractor, turning up a hill at the end of the field when the wheels of the tractor started to spin. He pushed in the clutch and brake in an effort to stop and back up, but when he did, the tractor began to slide backwards down the hill.

Soon he was picking up speed and heading for the bottom of the field. At the field edge was a steep slope covered with trees. Before he knew it, he was in the trees and bouncing around in the cab. The tractor came to rest about twenty feet from a ten-foot-high embankment which dropped straight down to the road. It was the last tree that stopped this from occurring. The manure spreader and tractor were demolished from the beating they took. He had cleared a path ten feet wide and seventy feet long. Thank God for his protection, for Stacy walked away with only one bruise—his pride!

THE END OF FARM LIFE:

In 1991, the Snyders made a decision to leave the farming life and start a new venture together. They purchased a restaurant in Sunbury, Pennsylvania, that they named "the

Augusta House." Although they worked hard at making this restaurant a success, the location was out of the way and their business failed; and sadly, so did their marriage. In 1994, Marvin and his wife went through a divorce.

ANOTHER MIRACLE OF PROTECTION:

In 1994, God protected Marvin again. He had a banquet scheduled on a Saturday morning at the restaurant. He decided to stay at the restaurant instead of returning home on Friday night and planned to sleep on his recliner in the office. At the beginning of the week, he had told Stacy about noticing a man standing on the sidewalk several times that week. It looked like the man was casing the place out.

They had discussed if Marvin should keep a gun with him in case of a break in. Marvin was a hunter and had a permit to carry a gun. However, after prayer, he felt the Lord saying to him, "If you live by the sword, you will die by the sword." He decided not to take his gun to the restaurant.

At four in the morning, Marvin was awakened to locker doors slamming. He thought maybe one of his workers had come into the restaurant early to prepare for the banquet. He saw lights through the crack in the office door and knew someone was coming into the office. He got up and went to the door and opened it and there stood a man with a bar in his hand. He looked like the Statue of Liberty!

Marvin ordered him out of his restaurant but the man just stood there in shock. He was not expecting to find anyone in the building. Since he did not move and Marvin had no weapon to protect himself, he called on God to help him. He pointed to the man and said, "In the name of Jesus, get out of here!" The man started moaning and bending over and looked like he was going to fall. Instead, he turned his light out and ran out of the building.

Marvin called 911 and the police came within minutes. Only $150 had been taken out of the open cash register, and Marvin had not been hurt. Marvin was so glad he had trusted God and did not have a gun with him. He believes that God surrounded him with angels to protect him. He was glad he did not have to live with the knowledge that he had shot anyone.

GOD PROVIDES AND PROTECTS JANEL:

After Janel graduated from college, she got a job working for American Home Foods. However, the time came when the company had to downsize. Janel found herself in the position of not having a job, nowhere to stay, and her car that was not working. She really needed God to help her. She made it a matter of prayer. Within one week, God opened up a good job for her at Geisinger Medical Center and also provided her with a car and housing. She declares that the way God did this for her was truly a miracle.

In 1993, she left Geisinger to travel with a Christian vocal group that travelled throughout America ministering to hospitalized veterans who had returned with severe injuries from the war. The group also ministered in churches and public places to get the funds to do this ministry. It was through Re-Creation she met Matthew, another member of the group.

On the way to their first big tour, they were involved in a terrible accident and their van went over an embankment. Janel was thrown out of the van and landed in a raspberry patch about thirty feet from the van. She thanked God for that bush that broke her fall and saved her life. Although hospitalized for a few days with a broken nose, scratches and bruises, she lived through what could have been a tragedy.

Matt was also protected. Although they had to use the Jaws of Life to get him out of the van and he had a severe laceration on his arm, he was protected from serious injury as were the other young people in the vehicle. God was good to all of them.

In 1994, Janel and Matthew were married and went away to a Methodist seminary and have been involved in the ministry since then. Today, they live in Ohio and are the proud parents of four children: Gabrielle, Samuel, Christian and Elizabeth.

AN END TO THE RESTAURANT BUSINESS:

After seven years of trying to make the restaurant succeed, Marvin had to abandon the restaurant business. He sold it and went to work with his older brother Jeff at Snyder Fuels. He had lost all of his assets and felt defeated in life.

One day after selling the restaurant and going through the divorce, he was standing by the Susquehanna River and crying out to God because he felt like such a failure in life. He felt God speak to his heart and tell him that if he would continue to serve God and put him first that he would again see God's glory working in his life. He was attending Brookside Ministries Church at this time and it was here that God ministered to his broken heart and healed his emotions and self-esteem.

THE SINGLES CLUB:

Since we had quite a few adult singles at the church, we decided to start a singles group. I said I did not mind working with the females but would prefer a man to help me to deal with the single men that would attend. Marvin was drafted into this position.

Marvin and I had so much fun planning things to do with the other singles that over the next eighteen months we became best friends. We used to deliver all the Thanksgiving baskets to those people who needed a helping hand. As a group, we met monthly to go out to eat together or partake in a planned activity we could all enjoy. Marvin brought laughter back into my life and I looked forward to the times we spent together.

I would try to set up Marvin with dates. He went on a few but, although he found the women very nice, he did not find anyone he wanted to date seriously. After he had gone on a date with a lady who had visited our church but who lived in New Jersey, he returned and I asked him how the date had gone. When he gave me the usual answer, I replied that I was glad that the date had not worked out because I would not want him to move away.

He said, if he did find someone else then our relationship would change, so why didn't I give him a chance and date him. It had been about two years since Louis had passed away, but I had never considered dating anyone seriously. I had been married for thirty years and had not dated anyone but Louis for over thirty-three years. Although my life's partner was gone, I somehow felt like I was being unfaithful to Louis if I were to date Marvin. I found out that this is a very common feeling that widows have after been married for a long time and then losing their mate.

Our church had a group that was going on a trip to Israel and I had been invited to go along. Marvin told me his sister Ruth would like to go and we could be roommates. Ruth and I became friends on that trip and I had a wonderful time. The three of us did things together and people started to ask Marvin and me if we were more than friends.

On our first date, I felt very uncomfortable. Afterwards, I told Marvin I just wanted to stay as friends and not date. However, we soon both realized that the feelings we had for each other had grown to be more than just friends. In June 2000, Marvin proposed to me and we got engaged.

GOD'S ASSURANCE:

We were happily planning our wedding when a friend counseled me to make sure the step that I was taking was indeed what God wanted for me. She felt that, since I had been in the ministry for thirty years with Louis,

I should probably be looking to marry another minister and that marrying someone without the same calling as I had would not produce a successful marriage. Neither Marvin nor I wanted to make any mistakes. I went to prayer and asked the Lord to show me without a doubt that the step I was about to take was indeed something he had planned for my life.

The Bible says in Jeremiah 33:3:

"Call unto me, and I will answer thee, and shew thee great, and mighty things, which thou knowest not." Jeremiah 33:3 (KJV)

The next morning as I offered up that prayer and had my devotions for the day what I read spoke to me clearly and, I felt the Lord saying to me that it was He who had put Marvin in my life. He had filled my life with joy and peace, and I was not to be swayed by others and what they may think. I was to trust God and be thankful for He was indeed fulfilling His promises to me. I felt He was telling me to rejoice and enjoy the moment.

I remembered the words I had heard the Lord say to my heart two years earlier when he had promised to bring new love into my life. I knew that this relationship with Marvin was of God and I had peace and joy return to my heart. I had no doubt that Marvin and I were to be married.

When the Lord had given me this prophecy, I remember listening to a tape by Dr. Yongi Cho speaking at a conference. He told a true story about a woman who had come to him during a series of meetings at her church and had told him she desired to be married. He had told her that she should make a list of what type of husband she wanted and post it somewhere. She should read the list daily and start thanking God for the husband he was sending her.

He said that God wants us to be specific with him. This woman did as Dr. Cho had instructed. When Dr Cho returned a few years later, she came running up to him with the news that it was not very long after she had started to do as he suggested that a young, handsome man who was a missionary had visited the church. All the young girls had tried to get his attention, but he had eyes only for this young woman who had made a specific list for what she wanted in a husband. This man later became her husband. When she checked her list, this young missionary had all the qualities she had asked God to send her in the one he was giving to her as her husband.

I had made a list just like she had made. I told the Lord if he were sending me new love, this is what I wanted: I wanted someone who loved God with his whole heart and would love ministry. I wanted someone who was a giver and someone who had a good sense of humor. I wanted someone who would love me unconditionally and who would love my children. I wanted God to send me one of his princes! God did just that when he gave Marvin to me and I thank him daily for loving us so much and giving Marvin and me a second chance at love.

THE END OF MY MOURNING AND GRIEF:

"To proclaim the acceptable year of the Lord, and the day of vengeance of our God; to comfort all that mourn;

To appoint unto them that mourn in Zion to give unto them beauty for ashes, the oil of joy for mourning, the garment of praise for the spirit of heaviness; that they might be called trees of righteousness, the planting of the Lord, that he might be glorified."

Isaiah 61:2-3 (KJV)

MY FIRST GRANDCHILD:

Jason and Renee gave us the news that they were expecting a baby, and on August 7, 2000, Blake Louis Correa was born. As soon as we got the news, we went to the hospital to greet the new addition to the family. Holding my precious grandson in my arms shortly after his birth was a reminder that life indeed goes on.

When Blake was born, Renee told me that he was blue and not breathing. After the nursing staff worked with him, he started to breath and pinked up. God was good to us all. God protected Blake from having cerebral palsy from lack of oxygen at his birth. Today he is a healthy, intelligent, active twelve-year-old who brings much joy to his parents, family and friends. Bradley Joseph Correa was born four years later and is a healthy active grandson who brings added joy to the family.

Jason and Renee are wonderful caring parents. I am so proud of the husband and father that Jason is. He spends personal time with each of his children and he coaches their baseball teams and is very active in their lives.

THE WEDDING:

On November 18, 2000, Marvin and I were married, surrounded by our parents, children and friends. We knew without a doubt that we had God's blessing.

God helped us plan a lovely wedding. Heather was very creative and rushed to my side from Africa to help me plan the wedding. She made all the decorations. Everything was beautiful.

Gylene, Marvin's niece, took the photos for us and my sons were ushers. Stacy was his Dad's best man along with Jerry Helman, who had become a good friend to both of us. My stepfather gave me away and both our mothers were still alive and attended.

Janel sang some special music and we had some joyful congregational singing. Heather was my matron of honor and my friend Nora was a bridesmaid. Gabrielle, Marvin's first grandchild, who was not quite two years old, was our adorable flower girl. She was supposed to throw out rose petals as she came down the aisle which she did. Then, she turned around and picked them all up again before making it to the front of the church where Marvin and the wedding party were waiting. My friend Megan from Nursing School had a daughter after she graduated from school and her name was Kerry and we asked her to be the guest book attendant. Megan took photographs of the guests as they came into the church and presented this wonderful gift of memories to us as a wedding gift.

Matt, Janel's husband, who is a Methodist minister, gave a short message and Pastor Jerry led us through our vows after we both gave a tribute to each other, expressing our love and thanking God for bringing us together. There were a few tears and a lot of laughter. My brother and his wife came from Canada and all Marvin's brothers and sisters were able to attend. It was truly a joyous occasion for us, and the best decision we could have made. What a perfect day!

It was the beginning of a new union and new love for both of us. Our desire on that day was, and is still the same today, "Each for the other and both for the Lord." The year 2000 was truly a wonderful year for us.

THE UPS AND DOWNS OF LIFE

"The thing that hath been, it is that which shall be; and that which is done is that which shall be done; and there is no new thing under the sun." Ecclesiastes 1:9 (KJV)

Marvin and I sold our respective homes and purchased a new home in Sunbury, Pennsylvania that fit our needs. And so, our life together began.

We had waited until the following year to go on our extended honeymoon which was to visit my sister and her family in South Africa. It was a wonderful holiday and Marvin got to see Africa and meet more of my family who had many stories to share with us concerning God's protection and care.

My brother-in-law, Abel, took us to a seaside resort near Durban. We also went to Kruger National Park on a three-day safari and saw many wild animals up close in their natural settings. We went to Gold Reef City and saw how the gold was mined. We had a wonderful time seeing the sights and learning about the history of South Africa. We met some wonderful people and it was great visiting with family. While we were there, Michelle, Heather's oldest daughter, shared the following testimony of a miracle that took place in her life. I asked her to write it down and this is what she wrote:

> Psalm 37:39 says, "The salvation of the righteous comes from the LORD; he is their stronghold in time of trouble."
>
> I firmly believe that my mother, and grandmother, and perhaps even generations before in my family that I never met, were devout and exemplary Christians who dearly loved and obeyed the Lord. And through this love and obedience, our family has found favor with God which will be carried through for generations to come. Even though we may live in a world filled with evil and treachery, and we constantly face many difficulties, our family remains blessed and is always under the protection of God.
>
> My story that I would like to share with you happened approximately fifteen years ago. I was working in a pharmacy, together with two young student girls, and it was only ten minutes or so before closing time. Several people walked into the pharmacy and kept the staff rather busy asking for cough medicine, and other arbitrary over-the-counter preparations.
>
> As the pharmacist on duty, and it was nearing closing time, I was quickly capturing the orders in the system to ensure that we received stock the following day. Next I looked up and one of the students on duty was rushing towards me, with the other student closely following her. Initially I was rather alarmed, but then when I saw immediately behind them was

a man with a revolver pointed at them; I leaped probably at least three meters far, right off the raised platform behind the counter.

We were forced into a little storeroom at the back of the pharmacy that was filled with boxes. It was there that our assailants took the jewelry that we were each wearing. The leader of the gang opened his revolver and showed us that there was only one bullet inside. And then he held the cocked revolver against my head. All I can remember is that I prayed and asked God to protect us, and could only think of my little daughter of two years at the time that could not afford to lose a mother at such a young age.

In the storeroom, I had my hands and feet tied with ropes, and then one of the assailants approached me with a towel to gag my mouth. I felt instantly claustrophobic and fell backwards tripping over a box. Since my feet and hands were tied together, I lost balance and my legs went flying into the air and almost knocked the revolver out of the gang leader's grip. I didn't think that I was gagged after all—thank goodness. But the assailants did not threaten me thereafter.

We never really knew how many people there were holding us hostage: Two men came in and took one student away (they took her to open the tills and take the money). Then a few minutes later, she was brought back and then some other men came in and took the other student's pants off. Then they led her away (afterwards we realized that she was taken to the kitchen where there was a safe and they tried to have her open the safe). She was brought back again a few minutes later. Then all the assailants left the room and closed the storeroom door. All three of us sat silently in shock. We did not dare to leave the room so we huddled together and waited. We thought we could hear the shop door sliding closed, but were too terrified to open the storeroom door to check.

It was after another few long minutes that we heard the shop door slide open again and a lady ask jokingly "Girls, where are you? Are you playing some kind of joke hiding away?" It was the mother of one of the girls who had come to pick her up. We were so relieved that our ordeal had come to an end.

Out of all this, I realized how God had protected us. We cannot always stay away from crime as it is so rife in Johannesburg, but God can protect us. So much more could have gone wrong—we were not injured (except for a few grazes from the tightly tied ropes and a bit of shock), nobody was shot or raped. Life is so short and we never know what may happen unexpectedly. We need to live each day as if it may be our last. I thank God for the wonderful mother that I had, who prayed constantly for the protection of her family and that through her, our family continues to find favor with God.

A couple years later, we returned to South Africa for another visit and this time Ruth came with us. We went to Kruger Park again so she could see all the wildlife. We thank God for protecting Ruth on that trip. She was sitting in the back seat of the car and she had her window rolled down part of the way and was taking some photos of the baboons that were gathered on the side of the road. Suddenly, this huge baboon jumped up and put his arm and part of his body through the open space and into the car. Ruth screamed. She thought the baboon was trying to grab her expensive camera which she held on to tightly.

Apparently, the baboon had eyed a banana that was lying on the back window and wanted that to eat. It grabbed the piece of fruit and was out of the car as quickly as it had entered. It was a very scary incident. We were so glad that God protected Ruth from being hurt as these animals can be very dangerous and deadly and that incident could have ended in a horrible accident.

After she was safe, Ruth joked that she could not believe the baboon chose the banana over her! She did, however, make sure her window was shut so no more animals could get so close to her.

My nephew Shane gave us a testimony of healing that he had experienced in his life which he gives all the glory to God for. The following is his story:

"In 2001, I left South Africa and moved to Phoenix, Arizona where my wife at the time was a nurse. She got a job at St Joseph's Hospital in their Neurological Department, which is renowned as one of the best in the world.

A few months after we arrived, I was working out at a local gym when I had the weirdest sensation in my head and instantly got this huge black dot in my vision that would not go away. Now just before we left South Africa, a famous celebrity there had died of a ruptured brain aneurysm and the only thing that I could think of was that I was going through the same thing. St Joseph's was a mile away so I decided to drive there which sounds kind of crazy but I didn't think I had any time to waste.

A CAT scan was done immediately and a hemorrhage was detected and although they were fully booked when I got there, space was made for me because my ex-wife worked there. After that, I was given an embolization and gamma knife radiation and since my treatment, I have had very few side effects. Had I still been living in South Africa, I am convinced that I would have died."

"But even the very hairs of your head are all numbered. Fear not therefore: ye are of more value than many sparrows." Luke 12:7 (KJV)

It is wonderful to know that God knows everything about us. He knows what is ahead of us in life and he goes ahead of us to make a way for us to be victorious. In Shane's life, he made a way for him to get the help he needed and allowed him to be in the right place at the right time to receive the operation he needed for his healing. Isn't God an awesome God?

We had many blessings from 2000–2009. To date we have ten grandchildren born in this time frame. All are doing well at school and they bring so much joy into our lives.

In 2002, Stacy was married to his fiancée Judy. It was a joyous occasion. They have their own excavating business now which God is blessing. Along with their four children, Nathan, Rachel, Laura and Mary, they are kept very busy. They are teaching their children the truths they learned as children themselves: to love the Lord their God with all of their hearts and to love their neighbor as themselves. They are actively involved in their church and are a blessing to friends and family alike.

CATHERINE LEAVES US:

However, life has its seasons and ups and downs, and in 2002 we had to say our good-byes to my mom, Catherine. It is so hard to say goodbye to those that you love so much. We are thankful that the Bible says:

"Blessed are they that mourn: for they shall be comforted." Matthew 5:4 (KJV)

God had blessed Marvin and me with wonderful mothers. We thank him that we had many years to spend with them and glean from their lives. Because of their love and the things they taught us, we are the people we are today.

In May 2002, Catherine had gone to the doctor because she had been falling quite often and had developed Parkinson's disease. The doctor was afraid that if she fell and hit her head, she would hemorrhage to death. She was on Coumadin and her blood was very thin and she only had a third of her heart functioning. It was decided by the doctor and my mother that they would reduce her medicine to thicken her blood.

Catherine knew she was living on borrowed time and she wanted to go up to Canada to visit Charles and Joyce for a vacation. Without saying anything to any of us, I think Catherine was saying her earthly good-byes to her loved ones. We took her and Harry on this last vacation. She was feeling much stronger and thoroughly enjoyed that holiday. We stopped every two hours so she could stretch her legs and take a short walk. She tolerated the journey well.

She told me how proud she was of her son and what he had accomplished in life. Charles and Joyce would take Mom and Harry with them when they went to Florida for a vacation in the summer. They would also come down to the United States to visit them several times a year. We would take Mom and Harry with us when we went up to Canada to visit Charles and Joyce and when we took vacations. Throughout the years, Heather would come to the States to visit or Catherine would go to South Africa to see them. These visits were highlights in Catherine's life as she loved to see her children and grandchildren. She felt blessed that her children always had time for her and remembered her on special occasions and called her often. We had such a loving close family.

On this last trip we took together, she told me how much she loved all her children and was so thankful for providing each one of them with wonderful spouses. She said she loved and prayed for all her grandchildren and knew that one day we would all be together in heaven and that the family circle would not be broken.

When she got back after this trip, she spent an extended time on the phone talking to her brother in England and to Heather in South Africa. She had visited England and Africa on many occasions but had been saddened that for several years the doctor had restricted these trips because she was on oxygen and the doctor said she could not fly any more.

The last weeks of her life, she let us know how happy and contented her life had been. After saying these good-byes, one day after, she was on her way back from going out to eat with Harry. She had her eyes closed and was praying out aloud and saying, "I love you so much." Harry says she was talking to the Lord.

She arrived home and got out of the car and had a massive heart attack and went home to be with the Lord she had just been talking to. I believe she saw the angels coming for her. God had allowed her to say her good-byes to everyone and then he took her to her eternal home. Catherine was eighty-two years old and had lived a full, happy life. On June 3, 2002, we said our earthly good-byes to my dear and precious mother, Catherine.

When I think of all I learned from my mother, the one quality that stands out is her faithfulness to God and her family and friends. Faithfulness is one of the fruits of the Spirit that we are to develop once we become Christians.

"...be thou faithful unto death, and I will give thee a crown of life." Revelation 2:10b (KJV)

In the second book of Timothy 3:1–5, it tells us what the world will be like in the last days.

"This know also, that in the last days perilous times shall come.

For men shall be lovers of their own selves, covetous, boasters, proud, blasphemers, disobedient to parents, unthankful, unholy.

Without natural affections, trucebreakers, false accusers, incontinent, fierce, despisers of those that are good,

Traitors, heady, highminded, lovers of pleasures more than lovers of God;

Having a form of godliness, but denying the power therof: from such turn away." 2 Timothy 3:1-5 (KJV)

When we look at our society today we see that faithfulness is low on the totem pole. Especially in America we see that people will do just about anything to keep themselves in the number one position. The motto today is "If it feels good to you then go ahead and do it." But God tells us that He is faithful and that we as His children need to develop this character trait.

When you look at our society today we see that church attendance has dropped because people would rather go shopping, have family picnics or be with their friends or attend sport events instead of giving their time and energy to spending time worshipping God. These events are not wrong in themselves but when they take the place of worshipping God then you have not given God his rightful place in your lives. No longer do we honor the Sabbath Day and give this day to God. People have put other things before God and this is what is meant by worshipping idols instead of being true to God.

They do not realize it but by doing these things they are breaking the first of the Ten Commandments that God gave to us, which is to have no other Gods before Him.

God has given every one of us gifts and talents but many Christians would rather be pew warmers than be active and give of their time to let God use them in their giftings. They have lost their love for the unsaved and are too lazy to work for God anymore. They want God's blessings without having to do anything on their part. They will serve God if it is convenient for them and there is nothing else to do. Faithfulness to God is not high on their list of priorities.

Divorce rates have soared because people no longer stay faithful to their vows. The devil does not want us to work out our problems. He tells us to turn our backs on anything hard and to go look for something new and exciting that will give us pleasure. The devil knows the heartache of divorce and the effects it can have on the home, family and children and he is delighted to see homes split up through divorce.

Many people find themselves heavily in debt because they have not stayed faithful to paying their bills and they have stopped paying their tithes and offerings and honoring God with their finances. They would rather spend their money on material things for themselves to make their lives easier. People want what they want when they want it and don't want to wait for anything. Lack of finances or misuse of finances is one of the main reasons for disharmony in a marriage and can lead to all sorts of problems.

Although life can be difficult at times we are to persevere and not give up. There is a saying that says, "A quitter never wins and a winner never quits." This must become our motto if we are to develop the character trait of faithfulness.

It is always a choice that we make when we are faced with whether we are going to stay faithful or not. If we depend on feelings and circumstances we will fail the test of faithfulness.

Being committed to God means we have to live a consistent life. If we want our lives to count and others to see what true Christianity is we must be faithful in our devotion to our God, our marriages, our families, our jobs and our friends.

If you want God to promote you in this life then you must develop this character trait.

David says in Psalms 12:1: "Help, Lord; for the godly man ceaseth: for the faithful fail from among the children of men." Psalm 12:1 (KJV)

What helps us to stay faithful is our love for God. If we are loving Him, thanking Him, praising Him on a daily basis, He will put a desire in our hearts to be faithful. The thing to do is to keep Him as our number one focus in all that we do and think.

The people that have influenced my life have all been faithful people. It is my desire when I leave this world people will say of my life that I was found faithful.

JONMARK AND SHELLEY GET MARRIED:

In 2005, Jonmark married his fiancée Shelley Richter. Shelley is a delightful young woman with a good sense of humor. Again, I am thankful to God that he gave me another wonderful daughter-in-law to love.

Jonmark and Shelley decided to get married in the Bahamas, and the family and a few friends went along. They had a wonderful wedding and we all spent a week enjoying the sand and the sea and seeing the sights there.

Barbara and Dick Richter raised their three children in the Methodist church. Dick taught Sunday school for some time and they were active in their church.

Barbara had several things in common with her new son-in-law. First, they share the same birthday; second, they both love chocolate cake with peanut butter icing; third, they were both raised in the same old orphanage building!

MIRACLES OF PROTECTION AND HEALING THAT BARBARA HAS EXPERIENCED:

Barbara was one of four children who came from a troubled family and lived in deplorable conditions. Her father was an alcoholic. After her mother left him, she remarried a man with the same problems. Life for her was a downward spiral. When Barbara was six years old, her two aunts reported their situation to the authorities and they were sent to the Odd Fellows Orphanage.

The orphanage had one hundred children housed in the facility, but Barbara said they were always treated well. She was grateful that she was not separated from her siblings and they could all stay together at the orphanage. Her youngest sister Sharon was only eighteen months old when she was taken from her parents. At the age of five, Sharon was adopted by a good family, but later Barbara did get to connect with her again.

Although they lived at the orphanage, Barbara and her siblings still got to see their biological family members. They did not feel like they were forgotten and she is thankful for the good care they received at the home.

The Odd Fellows Orphanage was a private organization, which only started to receive state funds in the 1960s. They had a farm and each child had duties to do. Barbara remembers working on the farm in the fields. It was there where she was taught good work ethics. They attended school on campus until grade six when they went into town to finish their junior and senior high school years.

When Barbara was fifteen and Joe was twelve, the orphanage had dwindled down to only twenty children left in it, so they were sending the children to other facilities. Barb and Joe went to live in Pottstown. Her sister Linda, who was five years older than Barb, had graduated from high school by then and left the orphanage. This facility in Pottstown was run by a lady who Barbara says favored the boys. She was very strict with the girls, but the boys had much more leniency. Her brother got the chance to go to college, but the girls did not get this opportunity.

It was in Pottstown that Barbara met Dick. She found out that they had actually been born in the same hospital just a few days apart. After graduation, they were married. Then, they decided to return back to the Sunbury area to start and raise their family.

God Answers Barbara's Prayers:

In 2002, Barbara got the news that she had breast cancer. Her mom had died at forty-nine with this disease and her one sister died at age forty-three. Later, her other sister sadly passed away at the age of sixty-three from the same disease. Barbara thought this was to be her destiny, but God had other plans for her. After surgery and radiation, she is a cancer survivor, still living today to enjoy in the company of her husband and family. I am glad Jonmark has been blessed with such wonderful in-laws.

> For my thoughts are not your thoughts, neither are your ways my ways, saith the LORD. For as the heavens are higher than the earth, so are my ways higher than your ways, and my thoughts than your thoughts.
>
> Isaiah 55:8–9 (KJV)

We do not always understand God's ways. God used surgery and radiation to bring healing to Barb's body. Whereas, in other cases, he can do a miracle of healing as was the case of Catherine's leg being healed. It is not for us to question God's ways. The Bible just tells us to go to God with our needs and then allow him to work out the situation in his way and for his glory.

So many times we try to tell God how to do his job. I remember one occasion after Louis had died and I was feeling sad and lonely that I had prayed and asked God to give me a dream or vision to encourage my heart. Well, I sat down in my chair and closed my eyes tightly hoping to get a vision of something. All I saw was blackness. No vision came.

So then I gave up on that idea and went to bed for the night and prayed God would give me a good dream. The next morning I awoke after sleeping all night without dreaming at all. I was complaining to God because I felt he had not answered my prayer and encouraged me the way I had been asking him to do, when the phone rang.

The call was from a lady in our church whom I did not know at that time, but who had felt led to call me and invite me out to eat. I felt so encouraged at the invitation. When I went to have my devotions that night, the Lord spoke to my heart and this is what he impressed on me. God did not send me a vision or a dream because that is not what I needed. He sent me a person to encourage me because that is what I needed.

Sometimes we try to tell God what to give us and how to do things and when he should move. But God is saying back to us, "Let me be God and do things my way because my way is the best way." He wants us to trust him completely with our lives and not struggle throughout life trying to figure everything out by ourselves.

To All Those Who are Going Through Grief and Mourning

Saying Goodbye to My Twin Sister Heather:

In 2007, I faced the biggest challenge I have had to face in this life: the death of my twin sister. My beloved twin had gone to be with the Lord. She had surgery on her shoulder and a blood clot had gone to her lungs. She had a massive heart attack and was gone. She was only fifty-nine years old and we had planned to have this big party at the end of the year over in Africa to celebrate our sixtieth birthday together.

I worked night shift. At the precise time that Heather died, I was at work and I got this feeling of nausea and my heart started beating really fast. After a short while, I felt okay again. Little did I know that, at the time I was experiencing these feelings, my sister had died. When I got home in the morning, my husband met me and told me the devastating news. I went into a deep depression and could not stop crying. I was so stressed out that my hair started falling out and I thought I could not live without her. She was part of me and I felt I was only half a person without her. Heather and I looked and acted alike and were like two peas in a pod.

I wrote the following tribute to my twin which I sent to be read at her funeral:

> This is the most difficult thing in life that I have ever faced. From the womb, you were part of me. We had a love between us that few on this earth have been blessed to share. For all the highs and lows and all the in-betweens, we were there for each other.
>
> Now, I come to try to say an earthly good-bye to you and I do not know how to do it. My heart is broken.
>
> I know that you are with Jesus, who you loved so much. Your life's work is finished. You are free from all your pain and you are in his wonderful presence forever.
>
> When I think of your life, I see a life shared with others. You had so much love to give. You forgave those who hurt you, quickly, and you had compassion for the hurting. Your gifts of encouragement and giving were so evident in all you did. You did not hide your gifts but used them for the glory of God. You truly were his hand extended to many. You were the best, faithful, loving wife to Abel and you often told me what a wonderful husband he was to you and how blessed you were. You loved your children and grandchildren passionately. I will take over for you, Heather, and pray for your family daily. One day I know we will all be united together in heaven with you forever.

We shared so much laughter together. Through my hardest moments in life when Louis and Mom died, you were there. We were able to lean on each other and strengthen ourselves in the Lord. Now you are gone.

The Lord saw fit to take you home and you are in a wonderful place and I know that the Lord greeted you with, "Well done, my child. You finished your course and now you can enter into your eternal home and be with me forever."

You will always be in my heart and with me. I have a lifetime of wonderful memories and no regrets. Our love for each other was complete.

I know God has a plan for me and that he will never leave me or forsake me. Right now I am at the lowest I can go, but he will sustain me. I am surrounded with a loving husband and children and family and many godly friends. No one can or ever will take your place in my heart. I am looking forward to the day when we will be joined together again in heaven.

I will always love you and miss you. I don't know how to say a good-bye to you on this earth so I'll end this memorial by saying, "See you soon, my beloved twin, my womb mate, my best friend."

Maybe you have lost someone or something that you loved and you find yourself in the position that I was in. Maybe you have lost someone through death or divorce, or maybe you have lost a good job or position or your freedom. You may be feeling devastated because you have made some poor choices in your life and now you find yourself in jail waiting for trial or have already been sentenced and you feel like life is not worth living any more. You feel depressed and do not know what to do about it. This is where I found myself when Heather died.

My mom taught me a great principle in life. It was, "You cannot always control your circumstances, but you can control your response." She taught me that no matter what the circumstances are in my life, God will not give me more than I can bear and that he has a plan for my life which gives me hope and an expected end. Through Heather's home-going, I have had to remind myself of these wonderful promises many times.

When Heather died, I asked myself the question, "How am I going to live my life to the fullest with my beloved twin not here anymore?" We had always been a part of each other's lives. Growing up, we were not even called by our own names but were known as "the twins" and we would make all our decisions in life together. I felt such a deep, deep loss that I believe only a twin can understand.

Through this journey, I have found out some important things. God does not expect us not to grieve. When we lose something precious, this is a normal human thing to do. However, he does not want this grieving process to go on forever so that it cripples us in life.

The first thing I had to learn in order to live a full contented life without Heather was I had to change my focus. I had to allow myself to grieve the loss. Then I had to dry my tears and concentrate on life here among the living and count my blessings. I have a wonderful husband, precious children and grandchildren who love me. I have great friends. I have good health, food on my table, clothes on my back, my home, a job, a little money in my pocket, etc. The blessings are so evident in my life. I was blessed with a love of a twin for fifty-nine years, something others have never experienced and I was to be thankful for all those years.

I have been taught all my life that if I kept in the Word, the Word would keep me from any storms I may have to go through in this life. Now was to be the test. I was to focus on God's ability, not on my own.

I once read a statement that was profound. It was this: Often God will not calm the storm around you but he has promised to calm the storm within you. Sometimes the circumstances we are in do not change quickly like we want them to, but he has promised to give us inner peace, joy and strength as we cling to him through the storms of life.

Life goes on. I found out that nothing is so hard that you cannot handle it if you keep a positive attitude and do it God's way. We can break free from bondage by coming to God in prayer and asking that the bondages, the lies of Satan, be broken. Those lies keep you from having a loving relationship with God. Relationship is so important. We are to make our requests known and trust God to do what only he can do. We are to confess his word, not our own. When thoughts of inadequacy fill our heads, we are to stop and remember that God's grace is sufficient to meet all our needs.

Once after Heather's death, when I was crying and missing my twin, I thought to myself Satan wants to rob me of the privilege of going to God because he wants to see me full of anxiety and fear and confusion. He wants me to have a terrible day. It is the devil who steals your peace. I did what God was teaching me. I refocused on the goodness and blessings of God and I just started praising God and speaking to him. He calmed me down and I stopped crying and God blessed me the rest of the day.

"Wait on the Lord: be of good courage, and he shall strengthen thine heart: wait, I say, on the Lord." Psalm 27:14 (KJV)

I have learned through the years since Heather has gone to heaven that we are to take a day at a time and live in the present. One day I will see Heather again and I will see all my loved ones who have gone on before me. Life is short and the time we spend here on Earth is like a drop of water in a bucket. Eternity is forever. God has helped me and life goes on. I try to do what God tells me to do in all things.

> "Finally, brethren, whatsoever things are true, whatsoever things are honest, whatsoever things are true, whatsoever things are just, whatsoever things are lovely, whatsoever things are of good report, if there be any virtue, and if there be any praise, think on these things."
>
> Philippians 4:8 (KJV)

MARVIN'S MOM, MARGARET, GOES TO HER ETERNAL REWARD:

In December 2007, we had another loss in the family. Margaret Snyder, the matriarch of Marvin's family joined those gone before her and entered heaven's gates. She was ninety-six years old and had lived a long productive life.

If there was one word that I think of when I think of Margaret, it is "joy." She loved to sing. In her last months of life, when she was confined mostly to her wheelchair and could not see that well, we would arrive at her home and often hear her singing.

In the tribute Ruth wrote for her memorial service, she stated that one of the precious memories she had of Margaret was the following: "Mom was always a happy person. She loved to sing songs. Some were silly and some were serious, and sometimes it was just a la-la-la-la tune."

"But the fruit of the Spirit is love, joy, peace, longsuffering, gentleness, goodness, faith, meekness, temperance: against such there is no law." Galatians 5:22-23 (KJV)

In our troubled world today with all the crime, drugs, lack of jobs, poor economy, house foreclosures, school shootings and wars and threats of war, many Christians have lost all their joy. Certainly if we focus on these terrible things in life, we will get depressed and fearful. That is why God tells us to take our eyes off these things. We are to give these things to God to take care of and we are to put our futures in God's hands.

"Casting all your care upon him; for he careth for you." 1 Peter 5:7 (KJV)

We are not made to be able to carry around the burdens of this world on our shoulders.

> "Then he said unto them, Go your way, eat the fat, and drink the sweet, and sent portions unto them for whom nothing is prepared: for this day is holy unto our Lord: neither be ye sorry; for the joy of the Lord is your strength."
>
> Nehemiah 8:10 (KJV)

I believe my mother-in-law knew the secret of joy and she enjoyed the simple things in life. She loved her family and would love to talk about the good times. She did not dwell on the not-so-good times. We can learn a lot from her outlook in life.

WE SAY OUR GOOD-BYES TO JEFF:

In February 2009, grief and mourning hit our family one more time. Jeff, Marvin's older brother, was killed in a vehicle accident. Jeff was eight years older than Marvin and Marvin looked up to him.

As a teenager, Jeff had been somewhat rebellious at times. Marvin remembers when he was twelve years old and Jeff was twenty, Jeff told him, "Marvin, don't follow in my footsteps. When Dad asks you to do something, listen to him and obey him. Don't rebel against him as I did, I was wrong." That word of advice carried through into Marvin's life and helped to shape his life into what it is today. Jeff made up for his rebellious teen years. Jeff and his dad had a good relationship when Jeff became a man. Jeff turned out to be a successful businessman who was respected and loved by all those that knew him.

What we have to remember when we lose a loved one is:

"We are confident, I say, and willing rather to be absent from the body, and to be present with the Lord." 2 Coritnthians 5:8 (KJV)

For the one who dies as a Christian, they have gone to a far better place. We have to remember that, in order to deal with the grief and sadness that comes with missing them here on earth.

Jeff was a helpful, protective, loving brother. He was fun loving and, like his mom, he loved to sing. He will be in our hearts forever, like all our other family members who are now waiting in heaven for us where we will all join them one day.

The miracle that we have learned from all the losses of life in our family is that God does give us the strength to go on and be happy again. Yes, God can bring joy and peace back into our lives. Each time we go through a trial, we can learn something from it that will help us to grow in our character and we can become better person. As we look back and celebrate the lives of loved ones that have gone on before us and remember the good times, it makes us want to live this life in such a way that, when we go on, others will be able to say we left our mark down here and that our lives were truly worth the living.

I was reading the Bible the other day and came across this verse:

> And they found rich good pasture and the cleared land was wide, quiet and peaceful because the people of Ham had dwelt there of old and had left it a better place for those who came after them.
>
> 1 Chronicles 4:40

This made me ask myself, *What kind of example am I being to others while I live on this earth and what kind of inheritance am I leaving behind for those who come after me and look at my life?*

How we live our lives not only affects us but it has a lasting effect on others as well.

> "He is in the way of life that keepeth instruction: but he that refuseth reproof erreth."
>
> Proverbs 10:17 (KJV)

I truly want it to be said of my life that I left a better place for those who came after me. I want to leave my children and grandchildren a godly inheritance of blessings because I lived a righteous life.

When I look back on my life, there are many times that I have failed God and I have had to ask him for forgiveness, as I am sure everyone else can testify to the same.

But it is not how we start out that is important to God. Throughout the Bible we see that it is not how someone started their lives off but it is how they ended it that counted. Rahab was a prostitute but she turned her life around and helped the spies who had been sent by Joshua to find out about the layout of the land so they could defeat it. She acknowledged that the God of Israel was the true God and helped them escape. She committed her life to him. Because of this she and her whole family were saved and we find her name written in the geneology of Jesus Christ. King David had committed adultery and murder but confessed his sins and became a man who wrote many of the psalms praising God in the Bible, and God said he was a man after God's own heart. Many of the disciples and followers of Jesus had shifty backgrounds but after coming to Jesus confessing their sins and receiving forgiveness went on to do exploits for Him.

So don't dwell on your past mistakes. Come to the Lord, confess them and receive forgiveness from him and then go on to be the best you can be with His help.

We never know what a day will bring, but we do know that everyone has to stand before God one day and give an account of his life.

"So then everyone of us shall give account of himself to God." Romans 14:12 (KJV)

The question we need to ask ourselves is are we going to be able to give that account with joy and do we have the expectation that we will receive God's commendation and we will hear him tell us well done?

We cannot blame others and their hypocrisy, sins and mistakes for what we do with our lives. We must make the personal choices and do that which is right in God's sight and be ready for when our time comes to stand before him.

Epilogue

Throughout this book, you have read miracles of broken lives and broken bodies being restored. You have read stories of finances being provided and miracles of protection. Today you may need a miracle in your own life.

"But as for you, ye thought evil against me; but God meant it unto good, to bring to pass, as it is this day, to save much people alive." Genesis 50:20 (KJV)

It is a fact that Satan wants to destroy mankind in every area of our lives that he can. Satan has his own plans for us. One of those plans is to send us trials that will cause us to take our eyes off of what God tells us and place our focus on the problem instead of the promise. He knows that when we do this, we will get discouraged and want to give up. He does not want any of us to believe that God can do miracles for us.

One of the biggest lies that Satan tells is that we are failures or that we are going through trials because God is mad at us and wants to punish us. Because none of us is perfect and we have all made mistakes in life, this is a lie that many Christians start to believe. Satan does this so he can get us discouraged and depressed. If he can make you believe that God does not love you and that you deserve all the trials you are going through, the devil has a victory.

He knows that when we start to dwell on all of our faults and past mistakes and sins, it will rob us of our joy in the Lord. It will stop our worship of the Lord. It will stop our work and witness for God. In order not to let Satan get a victory in this area of our lives, God wants us to change our focus from ourselves and what we may be going through and put our focus on what Jesus has already done for us.

The best way to do this is to look up verses in the Bible that show us how God has helped others who were going through the same difficulties we find ourselves in and see how God brought them through their difficult times. Then instead of dwelling on what we are going through, we can start praising God for the victory that is coming our way and start praising God that the adverse circumstance we find ourselves in at the present time is not going to last forever. We know this because of the promises God has given us.

"The thing that hath been, it is that which shall be; and that which is done is that which shall be done: and there is no new thing under the sun." Ecclesiastes 1:9 (KJV)

All through the Bible, we read stories of real people like you and me who have faced the same type of problems that we are facing today. As long as they clung to God, he brought them through the difficult season in their lives and then he blessed them after the trial was ended. If we continue to cling to God's promises through the dark times, we will be rewarded.

"Jesus Christ the same yesterday, and today, and forever." Hebrews 13:8 (KJV)

Sometimes when we are faced with difficult circumstances, we get so desperate that we feel we are not going to make it. We have been trying to do everything right but nothing seems to be working out right for us. It is in these circumstances that we are to remember the story of Job in the Bible.

Job was a righteous, upright man who loved God. The Bible says he would stand in the gap for his children by praying and offering up sacrifices before God for them. God had blessed him with great wealth and blessings. He did not keep it all for himself, he gave to the poor. One day Satan had a conversation with God and in Job 1:8–22, we read this story:

> Then the LORD said to Satan, "Have you considered my servant Job? There is no one on earth like him; he is blameless and upright, a man who fears God and shuns evil."
>
> "Does Job fear God for nothing?" Satan replied. "Have you not put a hedge around him and his household and everything he has? You have blessed the work of his hands, so that his flocks and herds are spread throughout the land. But stretch out your hand and strike everything he has, and he will surely curse you to your face."
>
> "And the Lord said unto Satan, Hast thou considered my servant Job, that there is none like him in the earth, a perfect and an upright man, one that feareth God, and escheweth evil?

Then Satan answered the Lord, and said, Doth Job fear God for nought?

Hast not thou made an hedge about him, and about his house, and about all that he hath on every side? Thou hast blessed the work of his hands, and his substance is increased in the land.

But put forth thine hand now, and touch all that he hath, and he will curse thee to thy face.

And the Lord said unto Satan, Behold, all that he hath is in thy power; only upon himself put not forth thine hand, So Satan went forth from the presence of the Lord.

And there was a day when his sons and his daughters were eating and drinking wine in their eldest brother's house:

And there came a messenger unto Job, and said, The oxen were plowing, and the asses feeding beside them:

And the Sabeans fell upon them, and took them away; yea, they have slain the servants with the edge of the sword; and I only am escaped alone to tell thee.

While he was yet speaking, there came also another, and said, The fire of God is fallen from heaven, and hath burned up the sheep, and the servants, and consumed them; and I only am escaped alone to tell thee.

While he was yet speaking, there came also another, and said, The Chaldeans made out three bands, and fell upon the camels, and have carried them away, yea, and slain the servants with the edge of the sword; and I only am escaped alone to tell thee.

While he was yet speaking, there came also another, and said, Thy sons and thy daughters wer eating and drinking wine in their eldest brothers's house;

And behold, there came a great wind from the wilderness, and smote the four corners of the house, and it fell upon the young men and they are dead; and I only am escaped alone to tell thee.

Then Job arose, and rent his mantle, and shaved his head, and fell down upon the ground, and worshipped,

And said, Naked came I out of my mother;s womb, and naked shall I return thither: the Lord gave, and the Lord hath taken away; blessed be the name of the Lord. In all this Job sinned not, nor charged God foolishly."

Job 1:8_22 (KJV)

I am sure as each of these calamities happened, Satan would tell Job you are a failure. Even his friends told him it must be his fault that all these bad things were happening to him and that God was punishing him. Later, when God allowed Satan to bring sickness and pain to Job's body and his wife told him to curse God and to give up and die, Job's response was:

"Though he slay me, yet will I trust in him." Job 13:15 (KJV)

At the end of this story, God told Satan that enough is enough and Satan had to leave Job. The Bible says God gave back to Job a double portion of what he had before.

He blessed him doubly! This is what God wants to do for us when we stay faithful to him through the hard times.

The only way we can do this is to stay in prayer and praise and in the Word. We are to keep our eyes on the Lord and not look at our circumstances. It is not an easy thing God asks us to do, but with God's help we can do it.

One day when the disciples were out in their boat on the Sea of Galilee, Jesus came walking on the sea to meet them. The disciples thought it was a ghost and were all afraid. Peter called out to Jesus and said, "If it really is you, tell me to come and walk on the water to you." Jesus told him to come. Peter stepped out of the boat and walked on water, but he started to look at the raging sea and started to doubt God. He took his eyes off Jesus and he started to sink. He thought there was no way out and that he was going to drown. But in desperation, he did not give up. He took his eyes off the sea and he put them back on Jesus and he cried out for help, "Help me, Lord, I'm sinking!" The Bible says that Jesus reached out and took him by the hand and helped him safely back into the boat.

The Lord has promised us if we cry out to him in the rough times and put our trust in him, he will help us. He may not take us out of the storm immediately, but he will take the storm out of us and give us peace. He will help us to know that he will never leave us or forsake us and that one day the storm will come to an end and he will then give us a double blessing for staying faithful through it all.

When we go through trials we must believe in 1 Corinthians 10:13:

"There hath no temptation taken you but such as is common to man: but God is faithful, who will not suffer you to be tempted above that ye are able; but will with the temptation also make a way to escape, that ye may be able to bear it."

There is a story told in 2 Kings 4 about a widow woman in the Bible that did not have enough money to pay her debts. Her husband had died and the people she owed money to were coming to take her sons away as slaves. She was desperate. She did not know where the money was going to come from. All she had was a little oil. She cried out to God and at the last moment, God told Elisha, the prophet, to tell her to send her sons to the neighbors and get as many containers as they could and to bring them home. He then instructed her to start pouring the little bit of oil she had into these containers. She obeyed the prophet and, as she poured, the oil kept flowing until all the jars were filled. She then sold this oil, paid her debt, and saved her sons from slavery!

God loves to work in the area of miracles. When we find ourselves in situations that we are unable to do anything about and things look like they cannot get any worse, we are to remember that God loves to work in this arena. So be encouraged because Romans 8: 37 says

"Nay, in all these things we are more than conquerors, through him that love us." Romans 8:37 (KJV)

I have found out in my life that it is not just coming to God once to request him for his divine help. It is continuing to come into his presence and letting him know of my needs.

There is a story that Jesus told in Luke 18, the parable of the persistent widow:

> Jesus told his disciples this parable to show them that they should always pray and not give up.
>
> "There was in a city a judge, which feared not God, neither regarded man:
>
> And there was a widow in that city; and she came unto him, saying, Avenge me of mine adversary.
>
> And he would not for a while; but afterward he said within himself, Though I fear not God, nor regard man;
>
> Yet because this widow troubleth me, I will avenge her, lest by her continual coming she weary me.
>
> And the Lord said, Hear what the unjust judge saith.
>
> And shall not God avenge his own elect, which cry day and night unto him, though he bear long with them?
>
> I tell you that he will avenge them speedily. Nevertheless when the Son of man cometh, shall he find faith on the earth?
>
> Luke 18: 28 (KJV)

What do you want God to do for you today? Do you need a healing? Do you need a job, or finances to pay a bill? Do you want someone to share your life with? Go to

God and ask him for the impossible. If you have the faith to believe, he will do for you what he has done for others.

Yes, God can! He can supply your needs and give you miracles just like he did in the Bible and just like he has done in the lives of the people you have read about in this book. You have to accept, believe, and trust him and you will be blessed.

God is able and he will give you the same miracles he has given others. Believe it today.

Matthew, Janel, Gabrielle, Samuel,
Christian and Elizabeth Darrin

Jason, Renee, Blake and Brad Correa

Stacy, Judy, Nathan, Rachel, Laura, and Mary Snyder

Nigel Correa

Jonmark and Shelley Correa

Marvin and Caroline Snyder

Caroline Riddell Correa Snyder

BIBLIOGRAPHY

Wilkerson, David. The Cross and the Switchblade. New York: Berkley Publishing Group, 1962.

Cho, Paul Yonggi. The Fourth Dimension. New Jersey: Logos International, 1979.

I found books by the following authors to be a source of inspiration to me and to build up my faith in God.

Joyce Meyer

Charles Stanley

Mike Evans

Joel Osteen

Kenneth Hagin

David Yonggi Cho

Jentezen Franklin